A Meditator's Guide

A Meditator's Guide

*Venerable Pramote Pamojjo Teaches
the Principles of Mindfulness and Meditation*

Compiled and Translated by

JESS PETER KOFFMAN

**ASIA
BOOKS**

Asia Books Co., Ltd.
Berli Juker House
99 Sukhumvit 42 (Soi Rubia)
Prakanoang, Klongtoey
Bangkok 10110 THAILAND
www.asiabooks.com

ISBN 9 7 8 9 7 4 7 8 4 1 0 2 2

Printed in Thailand
Distributed by Asia Books, Co., Ltd.
Book design and cover design by Chunnungsue

Visit www.jesskoffman.com to learn more about or contact the compiler/trans-
lator.

Primary sources of talks included in this book:
Preparing for Dhamma Practice (Feb 8th, 2013)
Levels of Happiness (December 7th, 2012)
Mindfulness in Daily Life (Sukhothai Dhammadhiraja University, April 29th, 2009)
Finding Peace in a Suffering World (May 30th and November 13th, 2010)
A Meditator's Guide (July 13th, 2006)
The Ways to Wisdom (January, 2013)
Life Beyond a Self (Suan Santidham Temple, April 6th, 2012)

Contents

Foreword

Meditator's Guide is a compilation from Dhamma talks given by Venerable Pramote Pamojjo, one of the most revered and adored meditation masters in Thailand today. Venerable Pramote has a way of transforming complicated and age-old teachings into simple directions for a modern mind. As a result of this and his ability to see intuitively what needs adjusting in his students' practice, Venerable Pramote has become extremely popular among the Buddhist faithful in Thailand, especially the young intellectual and professional classes.

Venerable Pramote's student base is an estimated 100,000, of which I am grateful to be one. This number is constantly growing as people continue to download his materials, listen to his recordings and are, as a result, seeing dramatic shifts for the better in their lives. Many, including myself, are experiencing a decrease in pain and suffering in their hearts and much more happiness from listening to his talks and practicing what he teaches. Now, finally what is known as the "The Venerable Pramote Movement" that is causing spiritual awakenings across Thailand can spread to the rest of the world through English translations such as this one.

A total of twelve talks were chosen for this book, spanning the seven years that Venerable Pramote has been teaching at his Temple and Dharma centre, Suan Santidham, in Si Racha,

Thailand. Each chapter has one or two talks as primary sources and also includes some materials from other talks as to provide readers with more comprehensive explanations of each topic. The talks in the book include teachings on the true meaning of mindfulness and how it is practiced, both in formal meditation and our daily lives. It also spans the entire scope of Dhamma (Dharma) practice, useful for beginners first sitting down to meditate all the way to those practicing at the most advanced stages. It outlines the different kinds of meditation and when each should be applied.

There are many subheadings in each section for easy reference. Each chapter is a comprehensive work of its own and the book needn't be read exclusively in order. It certainly is not intended to be read all at once as each talk is rich with wisdom and needs time for readers to digest. As readers develop their meditation and Dhamma practice, they are encouraged to read and reread the portions of the book that resonate with them at any particular time. The book can act as a very powerful guide along one's spiritual journey to enlightenment. Especially when there is a question lingering, one may be surprised to receive the answer upon opening any random page.

Venerable Pramote speaks in a friendly and non-formal way and there was an attempt to be as stylistically similar to his Thai talks as possible. He speaks primarily in his Temple, Wat Suan Santidham on the weekends to crowds of 150-300 people and travels across Thailand and abroad speaking to groups of up to 3,000 at a time. He uses the word "we" as a friendly and less accusative way of meaning "all of you", so the reader should not consider the use of the word "we" in this book to include the master as well.

If readers find discrepancies with any of the material in this book, please assume the issue lies with the translation and not the source material. Similarly, if there are any areas of Buddha's teachings that are not present or properly expanded upon, please assume this is the fault of the compiler. I have chosen all the material in this publication in such a way that it is a guide for meditation and Dhamma development. Venerable Pramote's focus is on the principles of meditation and such is the focus of this book. Though Venerable Pramote does use many Pali terms, speaks of scriptural texts and quotes the Buddha regularly, I have not included such information in this compilation as my intention for this book is one of a comprehensive guide in meditation and Dhamma practice, and not a scholarly endeavour for intellectual or comparative purposes.

The power of Venerable Pramote's teachings are not just in the words, but the peace and understanding of the consciousness behind the words. The teachings here in this book are extremely powerful and transformative as they carry with them the true Dhamma of the Buddha. As the translator and compiler, it is an honour to be part of this transformation process for all those who come into contact with this book. May we all benefit from these teachings and be part of this powerful shift in consciousness that is blossoming in Thailand.

JESS PETER KOFFMAN
September 12, 2013

Part One

PREPARING FOR DHAMMA
PRACTICE

1

Preparing for Dhamma Practice

BUDDHISM IS A FIELD OF STUDY

Buddhism is more of a field of study than it is a religion. In practicing, we are taught to rely on ourselves, and not on higher entities or anything external to ourselves. To practice Buddhism, we must study; we must be an observer. We observe ourselves much in the way a researcher who has a field of study observes his subject. The subject of our field of study here is our body and our mind and our objective is to see the true characteristics of them in our own experience. We must be the one to study our body and mind—no one else can do it for us.

Buddhism isn't just about going to temples and listening to monks chanting. This is just the extreme surface of Buddhism: the monastic rituals, holidays, wedding and cremation ceremonies, giving donations for good fortune or good karma, and so on. When we're interested in only the surface rituals, as are most people in Thailand, we're missing the point of Buddhism entirely. The customs and activities are just the outer shell. Of course an outer shell or skin is needed, but it is a shame if we never go deeper than that. The surface has to adapt to the people of today and to our changing times; however, the true essence of Buddhism never changes. The Truth is always the Truth.

Buddhism believes in the potential of the human being to be able to observe oneself and see Truth (with a capital "T"!). Seeing the Truth of the way things really are is called seeing Dhamma. Once a human being sees the Truth or sees Dhamma, he or she can be free from suffering.

THE WAY TO APPROACH DHAMMA PRACTICE

Now, if we want to understand the Buddha's teachings, if we want to observe our mind and body, we need to have an open heart. This means we need to have humility, recognize that we are suffering and accept that we don't know everything. A lot of us are filled to the brim, thinking we understand everything about life and understand what meditation is all about. Of course, if we are still suffering in some way, then we don't yet fully and deeply understand the Buddha's teachings. We may have read Buddhist books, listened to talks and have a conceptual understanding, but the teachings have not yet moved deeply into the heart, the place where Truth is realised. This is why one needs to be humble and not let a big ego get in the way. If we start by thinking that we know how to meditate, that we understand Buddha's teachings, we will not see the Truth. We have to put that ego aside and have an open heart to learn the true Dhamma and free our minds from suffering.

Many psychologists and psychiatrists believe that they understand the human mind, but we see so many of them come to learn about the mind from monks who correctly practice the Buddha's teachings. The psychologists believe that they understand the mind and the heart of the human being, but if they truly understood their own minds and hearts, they wouldn't suffer anymore. Yet they come because even though they are researching the mind of the human being, they are still experiencing stress and they are still suffering. They come to learn the Dhamma so that they can free their minds and hearts from suffering. If they practice in the correct way; if they listen and correctly practice the Dhamma, then it won't be long before radical changes can be seen.

Practicing correctly yields quick results. We will see changes within ourselves. We won't practice for 20 or 30 years and remain at the same level. If we practice correctly, we will develop regularly and the results will be obvious. As I travel across Thailand and abroad teaching the Dhamma, I can see already that many people are starting to understand the proper principles of Dhamma practice. They are now becoming true practitioners of the Dhamma. Their minds are bright and they are practicing correctly and reaping the benefits: They feel happier, lighter, more peaceful. They are practicing the right type of concentration and gaining wisdom in the Buddhist sense, which is a deep experiential understanding into the nature of reality.

When we come to learn the Dhamma, we must be fairly easily contented and not too greedy or goal oriented. It is beneficial to be of the mind that even if we work very hard, that whatever profit or benefits we receive from our hard work are enough to make us content. If we are too difficult to please, needing everything to be and work in a certain way for us; if our expectations are too high or if we are too much of a perfectionist then we will have a difficult time practicing the Dhamma.

If we want to develop our Dhamma practice, we must also carefully choose who we spend our time with. Often we develop similar behaviours to the people with whom we spend time. If we spend time with people who have negative behaviours, we will often adopt negative behaviours. We should choose friends who are appropriate for us and will assist in our development. If we are looking to be more peaceful we will benefit greatly by spending time with people who are also more peaceful. We must choose our friends wisely.

We may have friends who like the Dhamma, who spend all day talking about the Dhamma or about meditation or mindfulness, going from this temple to that temple, or from one meditation centre to another but who don't practice much. Without practicing, we will waste a lot of time. We need plenty of time alone. If we are talking with people all day long we end up with a very busy mind that is difficult to bring into Dhamma practice.

We need balance: we shouldn't stay in solitude all of the time and we shouldn't avoid people all of the time either. We shouldn't restrict our eyes and ears from seeing and hearing the world around us. We don't want to totally close ourselves off. In fact, we need to experience the world. We let our eyes see what is around us. We let our ears hear what is around us. We notice as the body and mind have their different emotions and movements. The eyes see something and a feeling arises. The ears hear something and another feeling arises. We can see the different emotions that arise in the heart. This way, even when we are in a group of people, if we understand Dhamma correctly, we can still be practicing.

MORALITY BRINGS HAPPINESS

The first area of training required when we come to Dhamma practice is to achieve a proper moral standard: a foundation in, or a sense of morality. If we enjoy hunting and killing animals, annoying or harming people, arguing and becoming angry, shouting out, stealing and taking advantage of situations or cheating, we are not going to have the type of mind that is comfortable with any formal Dhamma practice. Our mind will be too busy and restless, not comfortable with itself. If we have a proper moral standard it's far easier to be with oneself and to practice Dhamma with an open heart, with humility and honesty with oneself.

A lot of people think it's difficult to keep a sense of

morality but this is a misunderstanding. Actually, if we are harming, stealing, cheating, lying, cheating or intoxicated, we are under the influence of the defilements, the impurities that fill the mind. We cannot be happy if we are filled with greed, anger and desire to hurt or harm others. If we have a moral standard where we don't want to harm anyone or take anything that doesn't belong to us, we can be easily contented and we experience more happiness. We can see that morality leads to a general sense of contentment that greed, anger, cheating and intoxicants can never give us. Moral people are generally happier than immoral people. It's not really difficult to keep a sense of morality when we see that we're happier and more comfortable that way.

If we're lying to this person and deceiving that person, we have a busy and restless mind. We need to keep track of what we told one person and what we told another. We have to worry about protecting our lies and worry about getting caught in our deception. If we just told the truth all the time we don't have to worry about protecting anything.

It is especially easy for those who drink, take drugs or other intoxicants to break other moral precepts. We can be led into lying, and we can easily cheat on loved ones or harm them in other ways. We lower our level of consciousness so it's very hard to have any mindfulness or awareness while we are intoxicated or feeling the residual effects thereof.

It's easy to see that moral people are happier. If we have a moral standard we are more easily contented, more easily

ASIA
BOOKS

สาขาออกใบกำกับภาษี : CC21-KPS2
RECEIPT/TAX INVOICE(ABB)
Tax ID : 0105512004424
ID.: (05) C 11 030 9) 03232
No.: KPS-KPS2 POS1
shier: SUPRAKOTE   Slip No. : 69392753
Rcpt No. : 0720396658
te   : 02/10/2014   Time   : 10:21:22 AM

9990514634 ART OF HEARING HEAR	1	590
9747841022 MEDITATER'S GUIDE.	1	540
TOTAL PAID	2	1.130

D-BY

R   1.130

unt (Exc.VAT) = 0
 = 0.00
unt (Non.VAT) = 1.130

peaceful, and we can more easily develop in our practice. Moral people tend to be better meditators. It's easy to see why the first of the threefold training of the Buddha is a foundation in morality.

CONCENTRATION AND OBSERVATION

The second area of the Buddha's training in Dhamma practice is understanding and practicing samadhi or concentration. It is mental training. We can see in everyday life that our minds are busy and restless. We are always looking for things to make us happy or things to find pleasure in. We go to eat and we wonder, "If I eat this, will it be pleasurable?" Then as soon as we finish eating we wonder, "Now what shall I do? Watch a movie? Listen to some music? Call a friend?" Our minds are very restless, moving here and there, looking at this, listening to that, looking for things to make us happy and comfortable.

Of course, when we begin to practice, part of the training in samadhi or correct concentration is the ability to make the mind comfortable and calm. In order to do that, we just need to find an object, a wholesome or simple enough object that the mind is quite comfortable and happy being with. Some people watch the breath and feel quite comfortable and happy watching the breath, and so that's the one they should choose.

If we are somebody who is easily angered, it is helpful to repeat loving-kindness phrases like, *"May all beings be happy and healthy. May all beings be peaceful and free from suffering"*. Repeating a phrase like this can slowly help the mind become more calm, comfortable and peaceful.

For those of us who have a tendency to crave, it is usually recommended that we use the body as our object and watch the body moving, sitting, walking and lying down. A mind tainted with craving or greed is often moving out, searching for what it can get. It sees things and then wants them. If we bring our attention back to the body—seeing it sitting and walking—it's very helpful to steer the mind back to the body and feeling content within it. We're looking to find an object that our minds are happy and comfortable watching and to make our minds become peaceful with that object.

We are not looking to be stressed by holding too tightly to this object. We are just looking to find something that the mind is content being with and then eventually it will stay there on its own. That's the first type of practice in our training in concentration, the ability to make the mind peaceful and comfortable for short periods of time.

There's another type of concentration—the fundamental type of concentration or samadhi that is necessary to develop wisdom and free our minds from suffering. This type of con centration leads to what is called a stable mind. The first type of samadhi creates a mind that is temporarily peaceful to give the mind a nice rest. The second type of samadhi is a mind that is stable as the observer. The object of observation can be thousands or millions of objects. We aren't concerned about what the objects are. We are concerned with having a mind that is stable—the stable observer of everything that arises in the body and the mind. To make the mind the observer is what we need in preparation for vipassana meditation, the practice of gaining insight wisdom into the Truth. And this wisdom, in turn, will liberate ourselves from suffering.

What is the Truth that liberates us? The Truth is seeing that this body and mind exhibit the Three Characteristics: impermanence (the body and mind are always changing), unsatisfactoriness (in the body and mind, all states are under oppression by suffering and cannot persist) and non-self (ultimately nothing that arises in the mind and body is a self or under anyone's control).

Once we achieve the stable mind or the second type of concentration, then we will be able to gain insight into the Three Characteristics. This is developing wisdom, the third of Buddha's three-fold training in Dhamma. We will observe that everything is always changing. We will observe that suffering is oppressing the body and mind all the time and nothing in the body and mind is satisfactory. We will observe that nothing that arises or falls is under our control or anyone's control; that things arise and fall on their own according to their own causes and that there isn't anyone doing it.

BUDDHISM'S UNIQUE FOCUS

If we have correct concentration and if we have a proper foundation in morality, then the opportunity for true wisdom and freedom from suffering is there and will happen eventually. The Buddha taught us how to release our minds from suffering in a permanent way, right here and now in this lifetime. In order to free our minds however, we have to do what is necessary and appropriate, set the right causes for the right outcome. If we practice correctly, we will have great results in this lifetime. We shouldn't think that it will take lifetimes before we can be free from suffering. However, we have to practice the Dhamma according to our skills and our abilities and know what is appropriate for us at any particular time.

All religions have rituals and teach about keeping moral standards, about being a good person. What separates Buddhism from other religions is the teachings on how to liberate one's mind from pain and suffering once and for all. Other religions even have types of meditation. In the Muslim religion people think about God five times a day and make their minds calm, peaceful and faithful. In the Christian religion people come to church and sing together and their minds are content and concentrated with songs. Meditation is available in all religions. If practicing meditation and keeping moral standards is all we do, we become a quality person, but it's still not enough for lasting happiness. We have to practice the Dhamma until every last impurity has been washed away from our heart.

The key in learning how to free oneself from suffering is gaining wisdom into the truth of things. Most people are busy trying to make their minds still or peaceful for short periods of time, and in doing that we're not gaining wisdom into reality. This is the key difference between practicing Buddhism and practicing other religions: developing or cultivating this wisdom into seeing reality.

A PRECIOUS OPPORTUNITY

It's extremely unlikely that we can achieve enlightenment or the end of suffering on our own without a teacher. This is what makes Buddhism all the more important. We have our teacher and we have the community of practitioners and monks who have followed the teacher and reached the same state of purity, the same freedom from suffering. We have teachers and thus can be taught the way.

There are fewer and fewer Buddhist monks all the time and even fewer monks who are real genuine practitioners. These days people are even hired to become a monk if there are not enough available in certain areas where no one has volunteered to give up the material world to be with the Buddha's teachings. There are very few true monks who have spiritual attainments. This makes it difficult to receive true and genuine teachings on enlightenment and ending suffering. This is why when we are presented with the correct teachings and the correct way, it is a very valuable opportunity that we must not waste. We have the opportunity to listen to the pure and honest Dhamma that liberates us from suffering, so it's our duty to practice it.

Nirvana—the end of suffering—is something very real and very true. It's not just a fable or a story. It's something that we practice towards and we realise in our own experience.

Many years ago I traveled through Thailand and would see very old masters in their 80s and 90s—very elderly—and their bodies were deteriorating but their minds were bright, beautiful and happy. I would go into the city and see all kinds of handsome men and beautiful women looking wealthy, looking like they had everything, but their minds were nothing but dirty, greedy, angry, impure and unhappy. Then I would go see this elderly master in the forest and his mind was as bright and beautiful as it could be. Why was this? It was because he learned the threefold training of the Buddha. He had training in morality, in concentration and in wisdom and he practiced until his mind freed itself from suffering.

STRUGGLE NO MORE

Buddhism, this field of study into the body and mind, is very much a practice. Proper Dhamma practice has nothing to do with the posture we are sitting or walking in, whether we are holding a stick or beads, whether we are sitting very straight with eyes closed, or any such technicality. If we're able to see the movement of the body and the movement of the mind, it doesn't matter what our physical position is or what we look like when we are practicing. It's about whether we can be the observer, the knower, and see the movements of the body and mind.

Buddhism is also not just about being moral and watching the breath, or repeating a mantra and making the mind peaceful.

Rather, it's about walking the path of wisdom. It's about getting insights into the truth of the way things really are; what the true characteristics of the body and mind are. When we genuinely realise that the mind and body are impermanent, unsatisfactory and not controllable, then we will be released from suffering. We will have no more desire or craving with regards to this body and mind.

Normally without wisdom training, when a negative emotional or mental state arises, like sadness or boredom, we quickly try to do something rectify it, to change it to a preferred state. We'll turn on the TV, pick up our phone, indulge in dessert, or find anything at all that we think will distract or temporarily please us. We are constantly struggling, trying to keep the body and mind happy and comfortable. However, once wisdom that sees the truth and futility of these attempts, there is a happiness that is unimaginable and extraordinary. It is a happiness that doesn't depend on anything. This mind doesn't rely on anything to make it happy. It's happy in and of itself simply because it has released itself, liberated itself, from suffering. Such is the happiness and peace of one who has walked the correct path of Dhamma practice and meditation.

2

Levels of Happiness

There are many levels of happiness. Sensual desire, like seeing something, wanting it and getting it, is the lowest level. Better still is the type of happiness that comes out of samadhi or concentration. When we achieve peaceful states of mind through proper concentration, we can feel a more genuine type of happiness, a true rest. Then there is a higher quality happiness, that when the mind is the observer or knower of mental and physical phenomena. It's not the happiness of a small child just looking for pleasure, but the happiness of a true adult who is walking the path of wisdom and seeing the Truth. Finally, there is the extraordinary and unimaginable happiness of nirvana.

When we understand the truth of the way things are, this extraordinary type of happiness emerges. The ordinary type of happiness that arises from our daily activities like shopping or being with people we care about is extremely temporary and isn't reliable. It depends on circumstances and on people being a certain way, so it's very flimsy. We sacrifice our freedom with this type of reliance. We aren't free because we rely on our health, home or our loved ones being a certain way. We can't be free when we depend on circumstances, the outside world, people or things to make us happy. Eventually we all get old, get sick and die. For this reason, the body isn't a reliable source of happiness. Can we accept the truths that not everything will be exactly how we want it, or that we will be separated from those we love, or that this body gets old, sick and dies? If we can accept these truths, then we become more free.

We notice that the more we love someone, the more we suffer. Those of us who have broken hearts can see this. In the old days people used to say if we have a cow, we suffer because we have a cow. These days, we can say that if we have a car, we suffer because we have a car. In the old days people would have to wash their cows. These days we have to wash our cars. We have to wash this body of ours and take care of it. We do this because we love these things and we are attached to these things. We suffer as a result of our attachment.

For those of us who are married, can we feel that we've given up so much freedom? We may feel we do things and feel tired and bored or annoyed, or that we don't have the same freshness or inspiration as we once did. When our happiness relies on other people, we have to make those people happy. It's a happiness that's totally infused with suffering, responsibility and burdens. The biggest burden is the attachment to our own body and our own mind. Who here can see that the body is a burden? Who here can see that the mind is a burden? Earlier on in our practice, the body will seem more of a burden than the mind. Later, the mind will reveal itself as a great burden.

THE BURDEN OF HAPPINESS

Let's look at the body. Each part of the body has a vast array of products especially made to take care of just that area. Let's consider even just the hair. How many products exist to try and make us comfortable or happy with just that one part of us, just our hair? We need a brush, a comb, a shampoo, a conditioner. Some people have creams to make the hair straight, creams to make the hair curly, or creams to keep the colour a certain way or to dye it. There are so many things to do and take care of because we love this body and mind and are attached to them. The more we practice, the more we see that the things we take to be our self (the aspects of body and mind) are all a burden and a responsibility to uphold.

We're trying again and again all day long to try and make this body and this mind comfortable. We search out in the world for people to make us happy. We shift in our chairs to try and bring the body confort. The mind and body are always hungry for more pleasure or more comfort. The mind is always hungry for activity, entertainment and happiness. When the mind is hungry, we have try to find something to entertain it, to appease it, to fill it up and cure the hunger temporarily. The mind wants things to be comfortable, fun and happy and it wants to push away the things that are not comfortable, fun or happy. It always wants something. We can see that the mind is actually a greater burden in many ways than the body. The body is just hungry a few times a day. When we feed it, it's no longer hungry, yet meanwhile the mind is still hungry, always searching. Our attempts at trying to make the body and mind happy are futile.

To follow the mind and all its desires is tiring. The mind's cravings are endless. They even expand past our individual pleasures to those of entire communities. The mind engages with social and political causes and disputes, like we have with the yellow shirts and red shirts here in Thailand. If we look closely, we see that this is just the thirst of the mind trying to fulfil its never-ending desires. Just trying to make this body comfortable is a burden enough, and then we have to try to fulfil the desires of the mind too! It's a huge responsibility and a huge burden.

When the body is hungry, it just wants to be full. However, when the mind is hungry, it doesn't want to just be full—it wants pizza! It wants something fun or happy to fill it up and satisfy it. The body doesn't need much. It just needs a little comfort and a little food to fill it up. But the mind wants fun! How about clothes? The body just wants something to cover it and keep it comfortable, but the mind wants many clothes and certain styles. It wants choices. Our perception of what's sufficient is one-hundred percent the workings of the mind. The body doesn't want all that much but the mind wants vast amounts of innumerable things!

The Buddha taught us to just take what is sufficient. The less we want, the less we suffer, and the happier we can be. An enlightened being, an arahant, doesn't have any desires beyond just the simple necessities of life. Thus, the arahant is the happiest.

What do we do in order to wash away all this desire of the mind that is such a burden and causes so much suffering? The most superficial way to try and get rid of these desires, of course, is to do whatever the desire says. If the desire is to watch a movie, then we go to watch a movie. This is the easiest way, and it's what we normally do. If this is our practice, then we will see that there is no end to these desires. The fulfilment of desire is extremely temporary, so it's not a solution. Another option is to resist desire. If there is a desire to eat, then we ignore the desire. If there is a desire to do something, we don't do it. We restrain ourselves.

These two directions are both futile, the direction of doing whatever the desire says and the other direction of refraining from the desire. Instead, the Buddha taught to know. If the mind is experiencing desire, then know the mind is experiencing desire. Once we know the truth of the body and mind, we see that there is no way to make the mind stop desiring. It's the very nature of the mind to want, and it's the very nature of the mind to suffer. We believe that if we do what we want or get what we want, that we will be happy. All of the mind's desires are interested in being happy and comfortable, but trying to satisfy these desires is futile because there is no end to them, and no real satisfaction. There is no opportunity for lasting happiness when we harbour desire for a physical or mental state to remain in a certain way. If the desire itself is suffering and the mind itself suffering, how then can we expect to feel happier by merely obliging them?

HAPPINESS IN SEEING THE TRUTH

When we see the truth, we see that there is no chance the mind will be happy in any lasting way, desire fades away on its own out of this wisdom. Consciousness loses its attachment to the mind and to the body and sees that these are nothing but suffering and there is no chance of lasting happiness in them. Out of wisdom, consciousness eventually withdraws from them and desire never arises again.

The mind that has no more desire is the one that experiences nirvana and this state of enlightenment is the happiest state. The moment that consciousness sees the truth that the body and mind are nothing but suffering is the same moment that it withdraws, the same moment that desire or clinging is washed away, and the same moment that nirvana is experienced.

We don't have to pretend or fudge any results when trying to see that the body is suffering or the mind is suffering. We don't have to do that. The mind and body are suffering already, in and of themselves. All that we have to do is see the unbiased truth of the mind and body and we will know they are suffering.

We will no longer desire for this body and mind to be in a lasting happy state because we see clearly that this is impossible. When we have the wisdom that sees the truth of this futility, that sees the truth that the body and mind are of the nature to suffer, then desire will never arise again. There won't be any struggle trying to put the mind in any particular mental or emotional state. Consciousness will have let go of the mind.

ABOUT NIRVANA

It is very difficult to find anyone in this world who has genuine mindfulness as the Buddha taught it. However, once we do have mindfulness (as will be explained), it is not difficult to attain nirvana or enlightenment in this lifetime. Nirvana, the end of suffering for oneself, is something that is very real and very possible. If we don't believe that nirvana really exists, we are still very, very far away from it. Nirvana is the state where there is no more desire. Once there is no more desire present, we will know what nirvana is.

Desire is nothing more than our insatiable wants. Can we feel that there is always wanting going on within, one way or another? We want this one moment and want that the next. We are struggling to try to feel happy and comfortable all the time, and we never do in any lasting or truly satisfying way.

Nirvana is the end of desire. It is the end of ceaseless wanting. It is the end of fabricating a deluded reality. It is the end of mentally creating and perpetuating our own suffering. Nirvana is the end of craving for anything. It is not an external event or utopian society. Nirvana is real and is the greatest happiness. Everyone who tastes it feels this is true. It is free of the burden of upholding a self. It is free of attachment to this self. It is free of any mental impurities. It is free of suffering. But it is not free in the sense that it is complete absence or nothingness.

The Buddha not only taught that nirvana exists, but also taught the way and the practice in which we can enter the state of nirvana. Let's not form an idea that nirvana is something very far away, or just a mental concept of perfection, like a utopia. Talking about nirvana was not the Buddha's way of deceiving people into being good citizens. The Buddha's teachings are about moving even beyond good, not tricking people into being good. If we just do good, we may reap good things, but we will still suffer as good people. The Buddha taught us how to end suffering entirely and enter nirvana.

REAL HAPPINESS CAN BE HERE AND NOW

The way to reach nirvana is by learning oneself. The things that we call ourself are our body and our mind. So we must study our own body and our own mind, and come to see their true characteristics. Learning within our body and our mind and we come to see that the body and mind are just a part of world, of nature, and are not us. We can then let go of our attachment to them. Relinquishing our attachment to body and mind, we see nirvana. This is not as difficult as one might think.

This is also not a philosophy. Some people think Buddhism is a philosophy. Others believe it to be a science. I don't think it needs to be classified as any such thing. In all honesty, it is a field of its own. Buddhism is the study of how to release oneself from suffering. Once one fully understands this field of study, he or she will never again feel negatively, and will no longer suffer. He or she will live in this word happily without needing to find ways to avoid suffering. There will be no need to live in the forest or in solitude; one who understands the Dhamma is happy wherever he or she is.

We can be somewhat happy as regular working folk as well of course, but it is a matter of degree. Dhamma brings a much greater happiness for those who take the time to practice. Dhamma is not just for monks. It is universal, for everyone. If we learn to become aware of our body and mind, we will discover the greatest happiness, beyond what words can say and beyond anything imaginable.

Worldly happiness is fleeting. It comes for just a short time and then is quickly lost. Like when we have our eye on a girl we like, and finally get her affections. The happiness only lasts temporarily, and then we get used to her. We may even become bored. We will look for other things to try to make us happy again. There is no satiation point, no satisfaction regarding worldly happiness. It is very different than the happiness of Dhamma practitioners. The minds of practitioners experience higher and higher levels of happiness as their awareness of body and mind develops, as they get further and further from suffering.

Of those that have practiced according to my teachings, there is a vast number that now has genuine mindfulness and is experiencing higher levels of happiness. There are tens of thousands of people whose lives have changed. When they report on their experiences to me, they share how much their lives have improved. They used to suffer a lot and now they suffer minimally. They used to suffer for long and now they suffer only for short periods. Before they could be happy at times, but it relied on others or on a particular set of circumstances. However, now that they know how to practice the Dhamma correctly, there is a happiness within that is independent of outer situations. They are happy in the present moment, and don't rely on anyone to feel good. Happiness that depends on people and things turns us into a slave. We are never free. If we depend on someone for happiness, then we have to oblige them to keep them around. If we need a certain kind of expensive car to be happy, then when it dies our happiness vanishes.

We have the burden of continuously taking care of those people and things we depend on. Worldly happiness cannot compare to happiness from Dhamma practice. Each instant that there is mindfulness, there is also happiness. When there is concentration or samadhi, there is happiness. When wisdom into reality arises, there is also happiness. Eventually, when we let go of body and mind, an extraordinary kind of happiness becomes our experience. There is a higher level of happiness that awaits us at each stage.

The Buddhist faithful are very fortunate. We have a teacher, the Buddha, who has taught the way to attain liberation and this extraordinary happiness. We will become increasingly happier as we practice. We don't have to struggle for years and only get to be happy at the end. We don't have to practice in this life and only benefit in a future life.

Buddhism is quite amazing. If we have mindfulness, suffering that arises will instantly disappear right in front of our eyes. If we follow the teachings of the Buddha we will be able to liberate ourselves from suffering. The heaviness of life will be lifted, and we will be at ease, light and happy. The happiness remains as what happens in the world has no bearing on it. This is what mindfulness can do for us.

Part Two

MINDFULNESS IN DAILY LIFE

1

Mindfulness in Daily Life

There is no script or advanced planning when I teach the Dhamma. The teachings are expounded according to the quality of the hearts and minds of the listeners at any particular time. If the minds of the listeners are peaceful, the Dhamma that is taught will be profound and powerful. However, if our minds are restless, with our attention jumping around from this to that, the teachings will be superficial, and will jump around as well. Dhamma presents itself at a suitable level for the audience. Teaching about how to practice Dhamma is quite different from teaching Dhamma history or scripture. Teaching scripture can be organized in advance under topic headings and so forth. When I sit down to teach Dhamma practice, I have no idea what will come out of my mouth.

Someone, however, did title of today's talk as "Developing

Mindfulness in Daily Life," which is indeed the heart of Dhamma practice. Many people imagine that sitting or walking meditation is what is meant by Dhamma practice. They think that we have to surpass regular human behavior. For example, they may think we have to move very slowly and tenderly. They call moving and walking very slowly Dhamma practice. They think that if we sit in meditation we must keep a particular posture, close our eyes and not open them. They think that we must walk in a specific way and at a certain rhythm. The truth is that Dhamma practice has nothing to do with any of this. It is about having mindfulness. Whenever we have mindfulness, we can say we are practicing the Dhamma. When we have mindfulness, we can be said to be putting forth the proper effort. When there is no mindfulness present, then there is no effort and no Dhamma practice.

While mindfulness in daily life is the heart of the practice, this doesn't mean that we neglect formal sitting or walking meditation. We need a formal practice in the beginning in order to practice developing mindfulness. Once we have mindfulness, then we integrate it in daily life. Whether we make it or break it depends largely on our diligence in our practice in daily life. Those who only do formal practice have a very slim chance of reaping the fruit of nirvana, of enlightenment.

So how is it that we can walk the path that the Buddha laid out for us? We need to practice within the foundations of mindfulness (the body, feelings, mind and natural processes). We need to practice vipassana meditation.

There are two kinds of meditation: samatha and vipassana. Samatha we do so that we can make our minds temporarily peaceful, happy and good. In vipassana, we are not practicing to be happy, peaceful or good. Vipassana is about seeing the truth of the body and mind. We study the body and mind until we see the truth that they are impermanent things; that they are unsatisfactory; and that they are not who we really are, that they are not us (the Three Characteristics). When we see these truths, we release our attachment to the body and mind and encounter true and great happiness.

Unfortunately, there are only two main groups of people in this world: those who don't practice Dhamma and are totally lost in the world, and those who do practice but are addicted to samatha. For those of us who practice, we can do a quick review. If we have practiced for a few years and our mind can get peaceful, but then gets busy again; if it just oscillates between being peaceful and busy, busy and then peaceful, then we surely haven't been practicing vipassana. We've just been finding a place of peace and contentment occasionally. The peace or happiness of samatha practice is not a permanent thing. There is no lasting happiness in this world. We are content for a short period, and then the contentment vanishes.

Once again, samatha is about making the mind content, peaceful and good or wholesome. Vipassana is about gaining wisdom. Wisdom is seeing the truth of the body and mind. In the two types of Dhamma practice, the objectives are different and so are the methods. Therefore we need to be able to see the difference in our practice, if what we are working towards at any particular time is samatha or vipassana. If we can't see the difference, then most likely we will be doing samatha even if we think we are engaged in vipassana.

Many people like watching their breath and become very good at it. They are able to watch it continuously without their minds diverging elsewhere. If they think this is vipassana they are quite wrong. In vipassana one needs to see the Three Characteristics. So watching the breath with complete attention, or watching the abdomen without straying off to think, or watching one's feet during walking meditation, knowing every little movement, is not vipassana. Vipassana is not just watching the body or mind. The truth of the body or mind needs to be seen. This is not easy to understand unless seen in one's own experience. And one who sees the truth of body and mind regularly is on his or her way to the first stage of enlightenment.

Can we see that our minds are moving around from here to there all the time? As we listen to me speak here, notice that sometimes our minds move towards me. Sometimes they move to intently listen—they stop watching me and move to listening instead. After listening to a few words, the mind then switches to thinking, then listening and then thinking again. See? It moves around all the time, changes all the time. Once we can see this process quickly and clearly enough, we'll see that the mind (or consciousness) is arising and falling. It arises at the eye and then at the ear and then in thinking, all very quickly from moment to moment.

GAINING MINDFULNESS

Let's gradually become aware of the workings of the body and the mind. It is not too hard. It is much easier than we think. Firstly we need genuine mindfulness to arise. To practice this, we need to pick a type of meditation practice and learn to become aware. In order to see the truth of the body and mind, we need to at least come to see the body and mind. If we forget about the body and mind, then we have no chance of seeing the truth of them. So let's become aware. Being aware of body and mind is the beginning of our practice towards vipassana.

Normally, our minds are lost all the time: lost in seeing things, lost in listening to things, lost in thinking, lost in smelling, tasting and bodily sensations. For example, we can be sitting and get itchy. Then we go to scratch the itch and feel some relief. This whole process usually goes unnoticed. We don't see that the body is scratching and the mind is feeling relieved. It happens automatically and we totally forgot about our body and mind. Forgetting about the body and mind we can call mindlessness. Mindfulness, in the Buddhist sense, means knowing what the body and mind are doing. Mindlessness is forgetting about what they are doing.

Let's reflect on how often we forget about our bodies and minds. Notice that when we think, we forget about the body and mind. We cannot feel what they are doing. We have a body, but it is as if it is gone. We have a mind and it is as if it is gone. All we know is the content of our thoughts.

Mindfulness is that what sees or recollects what is going on in these Four Foundations of Mindfulness: in the body, in the feelings, in the mind or in seeing reality or the natural processes occurring within the body and mind. Put simply, mindfulness is what senses or knows the movement of the body or the movement of the mind in any given moment.

The first step in our practice is to achieve mindfulness. The second step is to practice in order to achieve wisdom. In order to build mindfulness we need to watch the body and mind and their movements. The body moves, and we become aware of the movement of the body. The mind moves, it goes off to think, and we notice the mind go off to think again and again. We build mindfulness and we also build correct concentration, a stable concentration that doesn't slip into thought or anything else. We have to practice to have mindfulness, stable concentration and wisdom.

WHEN MINDFULNESS SEES

Watch the movement of the body and watch the movement of the mind in order to achieve mindfulness. If suffering arises in the body, then we notice that. If we have suffering or happiness that arises in the mind, then we notice that as well.

Those who watch the mind, who observe the different feelings and emotions that arise, achieve mindfulness. They can also achieve proper concentration if they are able to watch the mind and see as quickly as possible when the mind goes off to think again and again. For example, if craving arises in the heart, then we know that craving has arisen in the heart. We have mindfulness in that moment. Then craving disappears from the heart, and we know that craving has disappeared from the heart and we have mindfulness again for that moment. So whatever good or bad, wholesome or unwholesome state arises in the mind, we know that it has arisen. When it goes away, we know it's gone away.

When craving in our example disappears, it's possible that there is no craving but there may be anger that's there instead, so we know that there's anger. Sometimes our mind or heart has no unwholesomeness in it. It's just a moment that we can say is the result of good karma. The mind works in successive moments, moving very, very quickly. In a moment when the eye sees something, there might be nothing unwholesome in the mind. There's just pure seeing in that moment. It's just the result of karma that we come to see a particular thing. In the next moment we may interpret what it is that we see and like it, dislike it, have craving towards it, or have fear of it. Then the mind is unwholesome again. If we can know the body and the mind in a continuous way, then our mindfulness becomes stronger and stronger. We achieve correct concentration where the mind is stable and able to watch whatever the body and mind do without slipping down into them. The mind is stable and rooted in awareness.

Mindfulness has the function of knowing what it is that has happened in the body or mind. We move and mindfulness knows that the body has moved. Something arises in the mind or the heart, like the mind wandering off to think, for example, and mindfulness is that which recognizes what has just occurred; in this case, that the mind has just gone off to think. If we are able to see this quickly and often then stable concentration or the observer will arise and we'll be able to see into reality without interfering with it. We'll have a stable, awake mind that is able to see what arises and falls. To walk the path of wisdom we need to have the mindfulness that is able to see whatever arises and falls within the body and the mind in a stable and unbiased way.

STARTING OUT

When we start off our Dhamma practice, the best thing for us to do is pick a home base for the mind as a place from which to observe what the mind does. If we are good at watching the breath, then we should choose that as the home base. We know the breath is moving in and out in a comfortable and easy manner.

For those who like to do Buddhist chanting, then do so in a comfortable and easy way. However, do not just chant so that the mind will become peaceful. For those who like watching the rising and falling of the abdomen, then choose that as the home base. For those who enjoy walking meditation, watch the body walk. For those who enjoy watching the body posture and positions, then choose the body. For those who like making hand movements for meditation, then let that be your home base.

We choose this home base so that we can know what the mind is doing. For example, when we are comfortably watching the breath, the mind will move towards the breath or the nose. Our job is to know that this has happened. The mind will also move into thought. Our job is to know when this has happened as well. If the mind is happy or unhappy, wholesome or unwholesome (good or bad), then know that this is so. Breathe and observe what the mind is doing or feeling. Or mentally recite or chant a prayer or affirmation and observe what the mind does as it chants. We may chant a few words and then the mind goes off to think about something else. We should know that the mind has gone off the chant to think. We may chant and start feeling at peace. We know that the mind is at peace. We may chant and the mind becomes restless and busy. We then know that this is so. We chant and notice the mind's changing feelings, moods and antics.

This is the practice to help us become mindful. We could equally choose the rising and falling of the abdomen. We watch and notice when the mind moves in and clings to the abdomen, when it goes off to think, and notice whatever else the heart or mind feels or does. This is what we should practice formally. We should pick a home base for the mind. It can be anything benign that we feel is enjoyable to be with. It could be the mantra "buddho, buddho" or any sort of chant. It could be the breath, the abdomen, the body's position, walking, or anything else we like. We don't choose this home base to make the mind still. We practice so that we can see the mind's movement, its changing behaviour.

Once more, we may opt to think the word "buddho, buddho,…" in our mind as a mantra. Very quickly, the mind moves to think about something else, and we know that it has done this. Then we recite "buddho, buddho" a little longer and the mind becomes peaceful. We are just to know that the mind is peaceful. Then we think "buddho, buddho" and the mind gets very busy, and we know this is so as well. If we choose the breath as our home base, then we breathe comfortably and notice when the mind goes towards or into the breath, when it goes off to think, and when feels joyful or happy or anything else.

We need to choose a home base as the main object to notice. Normally the mind runs around from thing to thing all day long. It is hard to see what it is doing. If we pick a home base then we can see what the mind is doing from there. If we have such a home, then we can see if the mind moves towards it to focus in, or away from it to think. We can see what the mind does more easily and clearly. If we don't have such a home base, it is hard to see what the mind is doing because it is so busy moving around all the time.

If we are not good at watching any particular object as the home base, then the best choice is any phrase to chant. Or we could even choose to listen to Dhamma talks on CD. When the mind goes off to think, know so. When the mind hears something funny and feels giddy, then know it feels so. When it hears something complicated and feels confused, know it feels confused. We should practice knowing the mental and emotional states in the mind as often as we can.

MAKING MINDFULNESS AUTOMATIC

Practicing to see the mental and emotional states that arise in the mind will help us to gain mindfulness. Mindfulness does not arise out of controlling the mind. The mind is non-self (anattā). No one can demand mindfulness to arise. Mindfulness will arise if the cause for it to arise is present. The reason mindfulness arises is because a phenomenon (physical, mental or emotional state) is well remembered. It is well remembered when we practice recognizing the state often. So we need to watch the mind often. We choose a home base, watch the mind move, and recognize what it does.

In practice, we may choose to chant and watch the mind go off the chanted phrases to think, again and again. The mind will begin to quickly recognize what this phenomenon of going off to think is like. When this phenomenon is well-remembered, mindfulness will arise on its own to notice the mind has gone off even if it does so for just an instant. Mindfulness arises by remembering phenomena well, not by commanding it to. This truth of the cause of mindfulness is very clearly stated in the Higher Teachings of the Buddha (Abhidhamma; TiraSañña).

Our job is to keep watching the mind until one day mindfulness arises on its own. When it does, we are conscious. We are aware. Once we are aware, the whole idea of different schools of practice—such as those that teach to watch the mind or those that keep to watching the body or breath—all goes out the window. Once we are aware, there is no choosing what to be aware of.

We may have the body, the sensations or the mind as a starting point, as a place from which to see the workings of the mind. Once we've practiced this enough, there is no choice what we will be mindful of. In any given moment there is either mindfulness or there isn't. Sometimes mindfulness recognizes a body movement, sometimes it recognizes a sensation, and sometimes an emotion. We have no choice in the matter. If we are only knowing within either the body *or* the mind, then we are moving out of vipassana meditation and into samatha. When genuine mindfulness arises, it does so on its own with regards to whatever phenomenon it sees in that moment, be it of body, feeling or mind.

WHEN WISDOM SEES

When I was waiting to speak today, someone came to me to report on her practice. She said she was showering or brushing her hair and she could see clearly for a moment that the body was not her. Mindfulness saw the body on its own with no intention for mindfulness to arise. It saw that she was not the body.

Mindfulness can also recognize a feeling or any mental state and see that that state is not us either. When genuine mindfulness arises, we will start to see that the body is breathing out, not "I" am breathing out. We will see the body is breathing in, not "I" am breathing in. We will see the body standing, walking, sitting or lying down, not "I" am standing, walking, sitting or lying down. The body will not appear as us. When a pleasant or unpleasant feeling arises, it will be seen as just something that comes in and won't appear as "I" am feeling unpleasant. When good or bad states appear in the heart or mind, such as greed or anger, it will be seen that the mind is greedy or angry, not that "I" am greedy or angry. We will see that all phenomena that arise in the body and mind are not a personal matter; they are not "me" or "mine".

Once we have correct concentration or a stable mind, we can see everything arising and falling in front of our eyes: happiness arises and falls, suffering arises and falls, anger arises and falls. When we are walking the path of wisdom, we can see that everything is changing, arising and falling in front of our eyes in our direct experience. We keep watching this over and over again and one day the wisdom will arise that all things are impermanent, unsatisfactory or that there is no self here or anywhere else. To do this we have to keep watching and watching the truth, seeing reality over and over again and one day the mind will accept the truth.

If we're watching the breath, for example, we can see that when we breathe out, it only happens temporarily, and then we're breathing in again. The out breath goes away and the in breath returns. The same is true for happiness, comfort, and discomfort in the body—we feel comfortable, then uncomfortable and then comfortable again. The mind is the same. The heart will feel comfortable and then uncomfortable, oscillating back and forth all the time, we see that no state is permanent. We call this impermanence, that it's there and then it's gone, it's there and then gone.

If we see that these things are arising and falling and they're not under anyone's control, or not "me" or "mine", we are seeing non-self. In our experience we will then see that all the different components that we believed to be us separate out from each other. They become distinguishable from each other—and we'll see that there isn't a person here but there's just a bunch of separate processes, like a body, sensations, feelings and an awareness that can be conscious of all these things. There is no person.

If we see from the perspective that none of these things can persist, that each thing that arises also has to fall, then we're also seeing the aspect or characteristic of unsatisfactoriness.

We've heard of the Three Characteristics: impermanence, unsatisfactoriness and non-self. They are all perspectives on the same reality or truth. If we see things from even one of these three perspectives, then we will gain wisdom into the true nature of things. We can't control what perspective will be experienced, either. It all happens on its own.

Once more, we need to start off by finding a home base that we are able to comfortably observe as a place from which to gauge the mind. Any object is fine. If we like to watch the body walking, then we should choose that. If we like chanting then choose that. Then we see what the mind does from there as much as we can. Mindfulness will start to arise and know on its own what the body and mind are doing. Mindfulness will sometimes see the body, sometimes see feelings, and sometimes see other mental behaviour. We will see that there is no us. The body is not us. The feelings and sensations, whether pleasant, unpleasant or neutral, are not us. The mental states, whether good or bad, are not us. There is no us. One with the wisdom that sees clearly that there is no me is called a stream-enterer. This is the first level of wisdom; when it is accepted that there is no self.

When we reach the intermediate stage of wisdom, we see the truth that the body is nothing but suffering. The way to see this is not by doing anything different than the earlier stages. We watch the body and the mind in exactly the same way we have been. Mindfulness sees what the body is doing sometimes and what the mind is doing at other times. Mindfulness works automatically, so we cannot decide what it will recognize.

We keep watching and one day the mind will have seen enough of the truth to reach a full understanding. It will come together and become very concentrated at one point. At that point it will understand clearly once and forever that the body is nothing but suffering. The eyes, ears, nose, tongue and the rest of the body are simply masses of suffering.

Who here can see that the body is suffering? For those of us that raised our hands, do we see that the body is utterly and completely suffering, or that it is suffering sometimes and comfortable at others?

We can see then that we don't yet fully understand that the body is always suffering. We see that it is suffering sometimes, not all the time. Like now, if we keep our hand raised, we will start to suffer! We can put our hands down now. *(laughter)*

So let's be careful not to hastily conclude that we understand the Dhamma. The Buddha taught that the body and mind are suffering. More specifically, the five aggregates that comprise body and mind (body, feelings, memory, mental formations and consciousness) are suffering. Yet we cannot see this truth until we have reached the later stages of enlightenment. Those that can see the body is nothing but suffering are called non-returners *(anagami)*. Those that can see that the mind is nothing but suffering are called undefiled ones or fully enlightened beings *(arahant)*. Everyone else sees that the body and mind are happy sometimes and suffering at others.

If we continue to have mindfulness, eventually we will see that the body is suffering all the time. There are only two possibilities: it is suffering a lot, or suffering a little. The mind will see this on its own. Once it sees does, we will no longer be attached to the eyes, ears, nose, tongue and the rest of the body. If there is no more attachment to the eyes, then there will be no attachment to what the eyes see. If there is no more attachment to the ears, then there will be no attachment to what they hear. If the nose is not attached to, then scents will not be attached to either. If the tongue is not attached to, then there will be no attachment to flavour.

The reason we are attached to the body, is because we adore seeing forms, hearing sounds, smelling scents, tasting flavours and feeling tactile objects. We are attached to these things. Yet when the wisdom arises that the body is nothing but suffering, we will relinquish attachment to all the senses and what they make contact with. There will be no more craving for or aversion to anything that is seen, heard, smelled, tasted or touched. This is the non-returner stage of enlightenment, the intermediate level of wisdom, where there is no more sensual desire. This phenomenon of no more sense desire arises from seeing the truth that the body is suffering.

ADVANCED WISDOM REGARDING THE MIND

Now I'll describe the advanced level of wisdom. Just like at school, learning the Dhamma has beginner, intermediate and advanced levels. At the advanced level, we see that the mind is a mass of suffering. Can some of us here see that the mind is nothing but suffering? Of course not. We haven't seen that the body is nothing but suffering yet, so we surely haven't seen this truth regarding the mind.

What we listeners here will notice is that we feel that the mind is happy sometimes and suffering at others. So we can see that we are not seeing in accordance with reality? One who sees that the body and mind (the five aggregates) are nothing but suffering, will wash away desire completely. Then no desire, attachment or suffering ever arises again. The cause of suffering is desire: the desire to make the body and mind happy and comfortable, and the desire to make the body and mind free of suffering.

Once we see clearly and directly that the body and mind are nothing but suffering, then we have no more desire to make them happy. Desire vanishes because we know that it is impossible to make the body and mind happy. Desire vanishes because we know that trying to make the body and mind free of suffering is futile. There will be no more craving and no more aversion to whatever arises of body and mind. There will be no more demands for the body and mind to be or feel any particular way.

The moment we see the truth clearly is the same moment that we drop the cause of suffering (desire). The moment that the cause of suffering is eliminated, the end of suffering or nirvana is realised. This all happens in the same instant, which is called the moment of the Noble Path.

Let's practice the Dhamma. Let's become aware of the workings of the body and mind. Let's observe that the body that stands, walks, sits and lies down is not "me" or "my" body. The body that stands, walks, sits and lies down is not us. Let's observe the workings of the mind. We observe it feel happy, unhappy, good and bad, and see that it is not us. It is not us that gets angry; the mind gets angry. If we keep practicing, we will see that there is no us in the body or the mind, or anywhere else. When we can see that there is no us to be found, we become a stream-enterer, at the first stage of enlightenment.

Then we keep practicing watching the body and watching the mind. One day the wisdom arises that sees the truth clearly: the body is nothing but suffering. All attachment to the body is then eliminated, including the eyes, ears, nose, tongue and skin. This, in turn, means that there is no attachment to anything seen, heard, smelled, tasted, or touched. There is no more craving for or aversion to anything contacted by way of the senses. It is the end of sensual desire. This is the intermediate stage. It is a stage where there is tremendous happiness in the stable awareness that is present. The mind is content in awareness and sees that the mind—that is thinking, making stories and fabricating a false reality—is suffering. So the work isn't done yet.

In the advanced stage, wisdom sees that the mind is nothing but suffering, whether it is in an aware state or not. The mind is let go of. It can be said that the mind is returned to the world or to nature. It is a miraculous event, and it is surely hard to understand how this happens. Let's just listen for now and keep practicing. One day this miraculous event could happen in our own experience. Once the mind is returned to the world, there is no suffering ever again. The thing that we are most attached to, the thing that we hold to be ourselves most, is our mind. The stage where the mind is seen as nothing but suffering is the highest level of wisdom.

At first, we practice until we can see that the body and mind are not us, not a self. At the intermediate stage, we practice until we see that the body is nothing but a mass of suffering. Then at the final stage, we practice until we see that the mind is nothing but suffering. This practice isn't as hard as one may think.

THE IMPORTANCE OF PRACTICING IN DAILY LIFE: MY STORY

I practiced since I was young, long before I was a monk. When I was seven years old, I learned from Venerable Father Lee in Samut Prakan province of Thailand. Since I was just a child, he taught me to practice samatha by watching the breath and to recite "buddho" as I did. I practiced every day. After a few years Venerable Father Lee passed on, and I didn't have a teacher to help me progress past my samatha practice. So I continued with samatha, making the mind very peaceful for periods. I did this for over 20 years and didn't progress at all. With samatha, no wisdom can arise to free the mind from suffering. The mind would get peaceful and free from suffering for a short time, but once the feeling would wear off, I'd feel suffering again. So then I'd watch the breath to make the mind peaceful again. If we only practice samatha, we just go back and forth between feeling good and bad, free of suffering and then suffering again. I had no idea how to practice vipassana at the time.

Finally on February 6, 1982, I went to visit Venerable Grandfather Dune in Surin Province. He finished his meal and came out to his balcony where I waited. I paid my respects and then asked him that I'd like to practice the Dhamma. He shut his eyes and sat still for almost an hour. He was very old and had just eaten... I thought he was taking a nap! I didn't know much at the time, all I could do was samatha meditation. I wondered when he would wake up and teach me. Finally, he opened his eyes and began. The first thing he said is that Dhamma practice is not difficult; it is only difficult for those who don't practice. He told me that I've studied enough books and it is now time to study my mind. This meant that I should start to see what was going on in the heart and mind. He didn't mean to analyze it, try to control it, or try to create any favorable state. He meant for me to just study it and see the truth of it. Whatever arises, we just know what has arisen. We are not to be the producer of what happens or a composer. We are not to be a critic or a director of the drama of our life.

He taught me to watch my mind. Before this all I did was watch the breath and body, but I didn't like watching the body. Now I was being instructed to watch what happened my mind. Well, I did what I was told.

At the time I was a government worker and worked Monday to Friday. One thing I noticed was that the moment I would wake up and recall what day it was, the emotions in the mind would change. When I would wake up and remember that it was Monday, the mind would feel lethargic and unenergetic. When I'd wake up on Friday, the mind would feel fresh and full of energy. However the mind would feel, I would know that it felt this way. If I'd wake up knowing it is Friday and feeling fresh, and then remembered that it was a long weekend, I'd feel even fresher. Does anyone share these sentiments? Everyone does! We wake up and think it's Friday and feel great, and then realise we were wrong it is only Wednesday! Oh, how quickly the mind turns to disappointment. We can see that suffering then arises. This is the way to watch the mind.

At the lunch hour, we go to the cafeteria and see they are cooking our favourite. The mind feels pleased. The next day there is nothing that we enjoy on the menu. We may complain, *"Why does this cook not think of something more original? It is the same boring stuff all the time."* Our mind has aversion. Our job is to know that the mind has aversion. Our job is not to know what food is on the menu today; it is to know what feeling arose in our heart.

We see a certain food and our mind feels a certain way. We smell a certain food and our mind feels another way. We know the feeling that arose in the mind (or heart) after it does. This is the practice of mindfulness in our daily life. It has nothing to do with sitting and shutting out the world. Wherever our life takes us that is the place we practice. So if we are selecting food, know what feelings arise. We may be happy they have what we like, and then taste it, and it isn't any good at all! Our emotion changes. Has this happened to any of us? We see something that looks delicious and then put it in our mouth and find it disgusting. And we feel great about that! I'm just joking. We may complain that the cook is lousy. Our mind is disliking, so we are to just know that the mind is disliking.

This is how I would practice when I wasn't busy working or having to think. I'd go for a walk at lunchtime after eating. I'd walk around and notice the mind going off to think, watching the body walking, and noticing impurities arising in the mind. When we do this we notice that whatever arises, does so of its own accord. No one ordered or planned what arose to be there. Things just come and go on their own. We just keep watching in this way, in a relaxed and comfortable way with no expectations and no thought to stop. We just keep practicing. If we don't enlighten in this lifetime, then we keep practicing in the next one.

Travelling to or from work, we get in the car and run into a traffic jam. We catch a red light. How do we feel? We feel frustrated, right? Then there's another red, and yet another. We start getting really annoyed. When we get greens, we feel glad.

If we hit a yellow light and have to break quickly and stop first at the red, how do we feel? Sometimes we get angry, right? Yet if we are the tenth car in the line at a red light, how do we feel then? Sometimes we feel even better than if we had to break suddenly and be the first! If we are the 50th car, we may feel totally neutral when we see the light turn green as we know we have no chance of making it. I hope it is becoming clear that Dhamma practice can be done in real life just like this, and real results will come. The main distinction between practitioners who reach the stages of enlightenment and those who don't is this: the ones who do, know how to practice in daily life. They do not overlook its importance.

It is a mistake to think that Dhamma practice is about shutting our eyes and ears and sitting in the forest. This is not necessary at all. Practicing Dhamma is about studying the body and mind and learning their true characteristics. We don't have to go to a temple to have a body and a mind. Wherever we are, are body and mind always there to study. So we can practice absolutely anywhere.

How many hours can we do sitting or walking meditation? Most of our lives are spent doing regular daily things. So if we only practice Dhamma when we go to temple or on a meditation retreat, or even formally at home for a short while each day, then we are not spending enough time at it. Most of us neglect our practice for the larger portion of the day sometimes in favour of meaningless and frivolous things.

I never neglected to practice when I was a working man. When I was a young employee and couldn't yet afford a car, I would practice at the bus stop. A bus would stop and be totally crammed with people. I would feel disappointed. Sometimes a bus would be coming with no one on it. I would feel delighted only to find that it was not in service. I'd have to watch it pass right by me! The delight would quickly change to anger. Of course the bus was empty in the middle of the route because it doesn't pick up people! It is pretty logical. This is a great example of proper practice in daily life. I see the bus coming and feel happy, then it doesn't stop and I feel angry. The job is to know phenomena, in this case, the feelings that arise.

In vipassana we have to see phenomena in the present moment. We have to see the phenomena arising and falling right in front of our eyes. If, for example, fear arises in the heart and mindfulness sees it, the fear disappears. We can see a moment ago the fear was there and now it's gone. We see it fall away right in front of our eyes. When the fear disappears just for a moment, the mind is stable and then we get lost in thought again.

Then when we get lost in thought, we get angry about what we think about. When the mind thinks something good or bad, it's not in our control. When we dislike someone very much, when we hate them, we think about them a lot. If we love them very much, we think of them a lot too. However, if we're impartial toward them, we don't think of them at all. Can we see that? When we're newlyweds we think of our partner all the time. Years later, when we are more indifferent to our spouse, we don't think of them very much at all. When our husband or wife is sitting across the dinner table and he or she has a new haircut, we don't even notice. We've become equanimous to our spouse! We used to think he or she was beautiful but now we find the food that arrives in front of us much more inviting!

This is the easy way to practice mindfulness in daily life, suitable for busy modern lives like most of us have. We don't have time to sit for long or do tons of walking meditation. Instead, we gradually get to know the feelings and emotions that are always changing. One moment we feel pleasant, the next unpleasant. One moment our mind is wholesome, the next it is impure. We are to just know what arises in the heart or mind, and we don't try to control it. We should not try to make the mind wholesome, happy or peaceful. We should just watch it changing.

Let's remember and recite what I'm about to say: *From now on, I am going to watch and see the changing nature of the emotions. I'll watch in a relaxed and enjoyable way.* Soon we will see that the mind is happy one moment and unhappy the next, good one moment and not so good the next. It just cycles around like this. Happiness stays just for a short period and then disappears. Discontent stays just for a short period and then disappears. Greed, anger, aimless thinking—they all stay for a short period and then disappear. Let's keep seeing over and over again that everything that arises in the mind also disappears. One day the mind will conclude on its own that it is the nature of all things to arise and then fall. This is a truth that the Buddha taught us to see.

One who sees this truth that whatever arises also falls in one's own experience, is a stream-enterer at the first stage of enlightenment. He or she sees that all things arise and fall, and so there is nothing that is a permanent self.

So let's practice mindfulness in daily life as I have described. Let's get to know what feelings arise and not refuse any of them. Let's know when anger has arisen, know when the mind is busily thinking, know when the mind is upset, and know when the mind is pleased or displeased. Let's keep working at this regularly.

Some people say it is hard to watch the mind. Actually it is really easy. Is there anyone here that doesn't know what anger is? Has anyone listening here never been angry? Has anyone never been greedy? We know what anger or greed are like. Do we know what a wandering mind is like? Have we ever been restless? Disgruntled? Sad? Jealous? Scared? Worried? We are feeling these things all the time! We know we do. Our duty is to notice whatever emotion or mental state has arisen in the heart or mind. If we don't understand what I'm talking about now, and feel a bit bored, then just know the heart (or mind) feels this way. But it is very rare indeed that anyone who listens to me feels bored! *(laughter)*

Can we all notice that when we laughed just now our hearts opened up and felt clearer? Can we also take note that at that moment we were not aware of our body and mind? Let's make sure to be aware by noticing the changes in the emotions and mental states as much as we can.

This is what my teacher taught me and what I practiced. I watched and saw that the emotions change all the time. One moment the mind is happy or good and the next it is suffering or bad. Let's keep watching like this and within days, months, or years, one of the stages of enlightenment is sure to be attained.

At each of the four stages, when the mind is ripe for enlightenment, the mind actually leaves the regular world for a few moments. In the regular world, the mind is moving around quickly from sight to sound to thought and so on. It is in the world of sense desire, looking for pleasure through the body and its eyes, ears, nose, tongue and tactile senses. This regular world is not where the mind enlightens. The mind moves into jhana, a high degree of concentration. Even if we have never practiced entering the jhanas before, the mind will do so on its own when it is ready. The mind then decides once and for all that whatever arises, also falls. It goes through a short process, and when the mind comes out of this process and back into the regular world, the feeling that there is a "me" disappears forever.

For all those of us who follow the Buddha's teachings, we need to make a goal. Let's be set on at least attaining the first stage of enlightenment in this lifetime. We should not think that it is too difficult to attain. Our duty is to cultivate the cause for enlightenment, and when the mind is ready enlightenment will happen on its own. The cause for the first stage of enlightenment to happen, where we accept that there is no self, is to have mindfulness that sees the body and mind as they are. Especially for city folk, it is important to watch the ceaseless flux in emotions. Then, one day we'll see that there is no us.

Let's give it a try, and see that it isn't as hard as we think. I've taught enough for today, so let me just summarize. Firstly, let's not let the mind stray away. Whenever the mind wanders, we forget about our body and mind. Secondly, let's not practice meditation in a stressed or forceful way. Let's not control the body or control the mind. Let's be aware that there is a body and there is a mind, and be careful of the mind that wanders off. When the mind strays, we lose awareness. At the same time, we shouldn't focus in or stand on guard waiting to see what happens. That is stressful and incorrect. We simply don't wander off and don't force the mind still either. We just feel what it is that is going on. We are aware of the body and mind and the changing emotions and mental states. We are aware in a light-hearted way. We just feel or know. We don't think about it and we don't force it or focus in on anything. If we practice correctly, one day wisdom into the truth will arise. If we exercise control, there will not be wisdom. Everything will become stiff and still.

Listening to me now, if we feel confused, we just know that we are confused. It is that easy. If we are confused, then we know it. That is the correct practice. When the mind wanders off, we know that it has. Let's not try to force it to stay put; that is an exercise in futility. No one can make the mind stop wandering for long. The mind is not truly under our control; it is not us or ours. So let's just know it over and over again if the mind wanders off. Let's know when the mind is happy too. Many of us now listening are becoming aware of their feelings and the mind is feeling delighted. We are to know that this happiness has arisen. Let's just know and not interfere with what goes on.

So, that's the practice. It is not hard at all. We will see that the Buddha's path to enlightenment is something accessible to anyone that wishes to walk it. It is not beyond the reach of a regular human being to arrive at this most worthy destination.

A Conversation with
Venerable Pramote

*S*tudent: *When I'm looking out at the world, I see the view much more than I'm seeing my mind. The knowing is just for a moment, and then I'm looking out again. Sometimes I am aware that looking is happening for longer. But I'm not sure if I am doing it right.*

VP: The way you are watching your mind is not quite the real thing. It is almost there, but you are watching too purposefully.

Student: Sometimes I look out, and I am not aware that I'm looking out. But I can feel that I am seeing.

VP: When you know that you are looking, it is not a natural knowing. It is still a little overdone, which makes it dull.

Student: Sometimes I want to come back to watching the mind.

VP: Don't do that. If you want to, just know there is wanting. Once there is wanting, see the wanting. That is watching the mind!

Student: I have trouble seeing the wanting clearly. I know I'm wanting, but I can't quite sense anything.

VP: Just that is enough. Know there is wanting, and then when it is gone know it is gone. It doesn't have to go further than that.

Student: The mental objects are often weak. I can barely see the wanting at all.

VP: That doesn't matter. Just see what you can. It doesn't matter which of the four foundations of mindfulness (body, feelings, mind, Dhamma) we watch.

Student: Sometimes when I come back to watch my mind, the wanting is already gone.

VP: If you come back to watch your mind intentionally, you should know that you are bringing it back. Here, greed has arisen; a defilement has arisen.

Student: When I intentionally come back to watching the mind, I know there is wanting to do it, but then the original mental phenomenon that I came back for becomes so weak that there is nothing left to watch.

VP: It is so weak because it is something of the past. That phenomenon has fallen away already.

Student: But the wanting seems to stay because it went unnoticed from the start.

VP: So how do you know then that you are wanting to watch the mind? That is the knowing we need. We don't need to watch wanting in any detail. We just need to know there is wanting. A few days ago a child was listening to me talking about seeing the defilements and asked, "When we see them, what do they look like? Do they have big scary eyes?" I answered that we don't see their body or shape; we just know when they have arisen. She replied, "Ooh, then I see them just fine."

Student: When I listen to you talk, I am still watching my mind too purposefully, right?

VP: Yes, a little overdone, a little more than natural. Can you see? Your mind is rendered a bit dull.

Student: If this is so, what should I do about it?

VP: There is nothing to do. Merely know it, just the way it is. Don't hate it either. If you do hate it, know you are hating it. If you want to fix it, know you are wanting to fix it. Just follow each phenomenon with knowing, as much as you can notice. In vipassana, we can only know as much as we are able to. There isn't a standard by which we need to follow regarding how many phenomena we need to know. "Shoulds" are just our own expectations. Just know what you can of whatever occurs naturally.

Student: I can't seem to separate my body from my mind.

VP: Because you still want a separation. I keep saying that we cannot make anything happen. Just know. Just know that you want the mind to separate. That is all you need to do. Separation will occur or not according to its own causes. What is the cause of this attachment? You are forcing the practice too much, as I have said, and it is making the mind dull.

Student: When I am looking out at things, does that mean I don't have an inner awareness? Does that mean I am "sending my mind out"?

VP: No. In your case, you don't totally let your mind go out. You are scared to let it out, so you pull it back a bit.

Student: Well, if I let it out it will stay out a long time; it will get lost in thought.

VP: Let the mind get lost. Then when it is lost, just know so.

Student: But it gets lost for so long.

VP: See? It is too long, right? It should be shorter, shouldn't it? There is the word "should" again. Too much, too little, too long, too short—they all come from our expectations. What can be done so that you are lost for shorter periods of time? If your mind recognizes mental states with precision, it will get lost for shorter periods and mindfulness will come in more often.

Everyone please consider what I say now as homework: Whatever method of meditation we presently practice, please continue it. Do it diligently. The only methods I don't recommend are those where we are watching something outside ourselves, like looking at a candle flame. These styles are not relevant to watching our body and mind. It is too difficult to come back inside and see the body and mind with such methods. If our practice is relevant to the body and mind, then please continue it. I recommend at night, we do our evening ritual of prayers or chanting and then do some sitting and walking meditation. We should do whatever method of meditation we are accustomed too, but do it to know the body and mental states. If our method is watching the abdomen rise and fall, likely we watch it as intently as we can in the hopes that we will benefit one day. Now we will make a little adjustment. Now as we watch our abdomen, if the mind goes off to think, then know it. If the mind is forcing attention somewhere, then know so. If the mind is happy, suffering, virtuous, non-virtuous, then know so. We keep watching and knowing the different physical and mental phenomena that arise. If we keep up watching and knowing phenomena every day, the mind will better remember them. This will enable the mind to recognize different phenomena more easily when they reoccur. Mindfulness of phenomena will then arise by itself. This is why we need to practice regularly.

Student: If I intentionally come back to watch the mind, then I am forcing it to, aren't I?

VP: Yes. That practice isn't quite right.

Student: But isn't that how I can watch and know mental states?

VP: That isn't knowing. That is focusing on the states. Watching the mind is about knowing what has arisen. This means that a phenomenon occurs, and then we know that it has. We get lost in thought, and then we know so. Anger arises, and then we know there is anger. Don't pull the mind back and set it to look. Just know after each mental phenomenon has arisen. Don't intentionally focus your mind in advance.

Student: So then how do we make the mind know often?

VP: It will know often if we keep noticing mental states as much as possible. We just live our normal lives. The eyes, ears, nose, tongue, body and mind will make contact with the world all the time. We can talk to our friends and do whatever else we do. Just know the mental states as they change. Eventually, the mind will well remember a great number of states.

Student: When we are watching, aren't we intending to?

VP: No, that is not true. Allow the feeling or mental state to arise first, and then know it. In this way, at first we will only know the really obvious ones, for example anger. Then later, we will know states a little more subtle, like being annoyed, and eventually, we will be able to notice even the slightest irritation. We don't force ourselves to see subtle phenomena arise; the way is to know simply and enjoyably.

This is what we all should do. Practice our normal meditation method, but when the mind gets lost in thought, know so. When it is focusing, know so. When it is happy, sad, angry, greedy or lost, just know each state has arisen. We train in this way every day, and make sure we find some quiet time to train formally as well. There need not be the slightest idea about when our practice will improve or when genuine mindfulness will arise. When we have had plenty of practice, our mind will remember many states and thus recognize them at once when they appear. Mindfulness will arise on its own in our daily life. In this room here, there are many of my students who have mindfulness arise on its own. And when it does, we will come to see the body is not us. It is just a form that moves. We will also see that the mind is impermanent, ever changing and cannot be controlled.

At this point, we will have learned what is necessary. And when we keep feeding the truth to our mind each day, watching the body and mind each day, one day true wisdom will blossom. It will be crystal clear that the body and mind are not us. We see more and more clearly as we sever the wrong view that the body and mind are us (There are ten "fetters" that are severed). We will then dislodge from them, and never have the feeling that the body and mind are us ever again. There is nothing to hold on to, nothing to maintain.

Let's keep practicing until one day we relinquish our attachment to the body. The mind will be completely and constantly awake without any effort. This is the Buddhist stage of enlightenment known as the non-returner or anagami. As we practice further, consciousness, the 'knowing' element, will show its characteristics of impermanence, unsatisfactoriness, and non-self. And the mind will let go; as it will no longer be anyone's possession, it will return itself to the world, to the universe, to nature. And then it is final. There is nothing left to do. We don't even need to call one who has undergone this process "enlightened" or an "arahant"—there remains nothing substantial to label or denote.

2

Finding Peace in a Suffering World

Thised with suffering, over-flooded with
it, in fact. When we are too young, we don't see this
truth quite yet. As we get older, we see the suffering of
all beings in this world, fighting for survival, status, harming
and infringing upon each other, fighting over lands, territories,
people and businesses. There are no beings that cause more
harm to human beings than human beings themselves. We are
competing, segregating, fighting and harming each other in the
most inexcusable ways, far more violently than any other being
in the world and perhaps the universe.

Other animals and beings on this planet don't segregate in
ways such as humans do. No other species of animal becomes
divided to the point where one says, *"You're Jewish, so we must
kill you"*. No other being is capable of the evils that humans

are. Humans rob entire species or cultures of life and existence. People of different religions kill or want to kill each other. Even people of the same religion but practicing in different ways want to harm or kill each other. Human beings want and need everything according to their image of perfection, according to their ideas and opinions.

Even in this world so filled with pain and hostility, we must learn to exist in it in an intelligent way. We have to see the truth that our greatest enemies are the impurities in our own heart; they are the things that prevent us from being happy. Other people can do many things and create difficult situations for us but it is only the impurities and defilements in our own heart that have the ability to make us suffer.

We all hate suffering. For example, whenever we give to charity or pray we always wish, *"May we be spared from suffering. May our loved one be spared from pain."* When we wish in this way we don't realise that we are actually asking to be far from enlightenment, far from nirvana. In order to attain nirvana, we need to know suffering, and to do this we need to see or experience suffering for ourselves.

What is suffering? The body and mind are suffering . More specifically, the five aggregates that comprise body and mind are suffering. The reason why we are not able to release from suffering or the five aggregates is because we still believe these five aggregates that comprise the body and mind are happy things. If we understand a little more than that, we believe that these five aggregates are things that are happy sometimes and not happy at other times. Take this body, for example. We see that it's happy sometimes and not at other times. We don't see that it's always just a mass of suffering, all the time. Similarly, the mind appears to be happy sometimes and unhappy at other times.

If we could choose between being happy or unhappy, we would always choose against being unhappy, against suffering, and choose to be happy. Most of the time in our daily life, we are consumed by ways to avoid suffering and trying to be in a state of happiness. We're struggling and trying to create stories in order to escape from suffering and stay in a state of happiness. Unfortunately, we won't be able to make the five aggregates happy or help them escape from suffering because suffering is actually what they are. They are suffering, proper. How can we make something not be itself? We see in this way that there is no chance of lasting happiness when we are attached to the five aggregates.

The Buddha took many years and endured a great deal of struggle and difficulty until he enlightened and saw how simple the Truth is. He already struggled and taught us what we need to do very easily and simply, so we don't have to struggle like he did. We can just learn from his teachings and practice correctly.

When it comes to practicing the Dhamma, we often ask what to do to make our minds good, what to do to be a good practitioner, what to do to practice correctly, or what to do to become enlightened. We always have the words *"to do"* in our consciousness. Instead, the Buddha taught us "to know". What did Buddha teach us to know? He taught us to know suffering. What is suffering? Our body and mind—the five aggregates—are what he calls suffering. It is the first of his Four Noble Truths, the truth of suffering. We start by knowing suffering within this body and within this mind.

When the Buddha taught to know suffering, he didn't mean to look at pain. Rather, he was referring to the five aggregates as suffering and he meant to look at the body and the mind, and to know the mental and physical phenomena that are arising or are present in this moment. We know within this body, know within the pleasant and unpleasant and neutral feelings, know within the wholesome and unwholesome mental states and emotions, know within this consciousness. Consciousness is always changing states: from thinking to knowing then thinking again, lost in the senses, or lost focusing in on an object. We see the phenomena that occur, and we'll see that the aggregates are always changing, always in a state of flux.

There isn't anything that arises that is stable and unchanging. It's like we're stuck to someone that is very unpredictable, inconsistent or fickle. Where's the happiness or contentment in being fickle all the time, constantly wanting this or needing that in order to feel good? In this way the aggregates are extremely fickle and because of this, suffering is their very nature.

THE FOUR NOBLE TRUTHS IN AN INSTANT

The Four Noble Truths: suffering, its cause (desire), its cessation (nirvana) and the path to its cessation (the noble path).

In the moment that we come to realise, to experience the truth of suffering, we become enlightened. We release from the cause of suffering and enlighten in that same moment. It happens automatically. When we see the truth of suffering, the cause of suffering is abandoned and the cessation of suffering is realised in that moment; the moment when the noble path arises.

The more that we practice the Dhamma the way the Buddha taught, the more eloquent we see that it is. However, when we don't practice the Dhamma correctly and listen to the Buddha's teachings, we become a philosopher or a critic. When we actually do practice correctly and see the results, it is truly life-changing. Who would have thought that when we see suffering clearly and directly, that suffering is then released, and that the cause of suffering is abandoned? Who would know that when the cause of suffering is abandoned, then the cessation of suffering occurs, that the noble path occurs? Who would know these things? All we have in this world are people who absolutely hate suffering, who are terrified of suffering. The world is full of people who are filled with desire, wanting not to suffer, wanting to be free of suffering. The Buddha was different. He didn't teach us to want to be rid of suffering; he taught us to know suffering. When we know suffering with utter clarity, we attain "the fruit of the path".

It doesn't seem to matter how well we take care of our body or how well we take care of our mind. One day they are certain to deteriorate, right? We can use this cream or that cream for our face but no matter what we do, or how hard we try, one day our face is surely going to be old and wrinkled.

We will get sick, we will get old and we will die, no matter what we try to do to these five aggregates. We try to take the mind here and there. We give it this food for fun or go to that place for entertainment. In the end we die and that fun, entertainment and happiness dies along with us. Can we truly have happiness by being attached and involved with all these changes that are going on with the body and mind, in the five aggregates? No. There isn't any true lasting happiness that comes from being attached to these things.

Just like the Buddha taught, through correct practice our wisdom will fully develop and we will see clearly that the five aggregates are nothing but suffering. This suffering will be seen from three perspectives. It can be seen because the aggregates are always changing and impermanent. It can also be seen because the aggregates are under stress or oppression, never satisfied and struggling. It can also be seen because no real self can be made out of them; the aggregates are not us.

When one of these perspectives on the five aggregates, on the body and mind, is realised, then the practitioner releases from the five aggregates and becomes an enlightened being. When the body and mind are released then this enlightened being, the arahant, no longer has any desire to try to make these five aggregates happy things. The arahant knows these things are suffering and that there is no way to make them truly happy. He or she recognizes this clearly.

The five aggregates are suffering. It doesn't matter what we do, they still suffer. When one has come to peace with this, to the full realisation of this, there will be no desire to try and make the five aggregates free from suffering anymore.

We can see in our mind there is an overabundance of wants and desires. We want this and that; we want a new phone, new clothes and so on. Underneath all of this, we mainly want this body and this mind to feel happy and we want them to not feel pain and suffering.

If we don't have a car, we feel it would be so much better if we had a car. The body would then feel more comfortable and happy. We are trying to make the body feel happy. Even if we had a car, we would then see others who had nicer cars, then we would struggle with that as well. This is not trying to make the body happy, but trying to make the mind happy. Soon we realise that the body and mind are nothing but suffering, no matter what physical and mental phenomena arise. None of them are anything but suffering. Whatever arises is suffering, whatever sustains is suffering and whatever falls away is also suffering. Other than suffering, there is nothing that arises and falls. When we see this, we realise this truth then we will have no desire to make the mind and body happy anymore. We will be free from desire.

When there is no more desire to make the five aggregates happy because we clearly see that it's impossible, then, of course, there is no more struggle. In the same moment that suffering is fully understood in this way, desire, which is the cause of suffering, is extinguished. At that moment, there is no more desire and there is nothing to be abandoned because it has already vanished.

We can see that we here have not yet fully realised that the five aggregates are suffering because we are still trying to find ways to make them happy. The complete abandonment of desire upon realising the truth of suffering is the complete end of suffering, extinguished, never to return. It's called the cessation of suffering, or nirvana.

The extinguishing of all desire is the exact moment that is considered fruition of the noble path, the moment that nirvana is realised. After this there will be no more creating fictions and stories, no more forming of painful emotions—the mind no longer abides in any realm at all. There are no boundaries, no limitations and we are free of all conditioning. It's the end of any burden or sense of responsibility in this world. All of these things are lifted.

True happiness or peace all happens in that one moment that desire is abandoned, suffering is understood and the cessation of suffering is realised. It all happens in the same moment and it all happens as a result of our practice. Then we become an extraordinary human being. To be this extraordinary human being, we must practice. No one can reach the noble path for us. We have to do this practice on our own.

THE STRUGGLING MIND

Those of us with the opportunity to listen to this talk are fortunate; we have enough to eat and we have proper shelter. We don't need to worry about the bare necessities of survival. Although we may be rich compared to most of the world, we still may not be rich in Dhamma. In fact, some of the monks upcountry who don't even have robes but through your donations, are given robes from my temple, can be far more rich in Dhamma, or far more rich in understanding the truth. This is because those who are poor can often see the truth of suffering more clearly.

The Dhamma of the Buddha holds no prejudice against any race, religion or social class. No matter who we are or where we come from, the Dhamma is available to all. It washes the pain and impurities right out of our hearts and it protects us from the pain and difficulties that are found in this world. This world is a place where happiness is elusive but when we have the Dhamma in our hearts, we have a lasting happiness, a true happiness. The Dhamma of the Buddha is all about our own heart and our own mind. That's what it all comes down to.

Today someone who donated monks' robes came to me and said, *"My mind is so busy. What should I do about this?"* The mind being busy is something that we are aware of using our own mind, correct? The mind is that which knows that the mind is busy. Once the mind is aware of an object, in this case the busyness or restlessness, we have to then become aware of the reaction or the relationship to this object. If the mind is very busy and we see that the mind is busy, there's a reaction that arises. It may be that we're not liking that it is busy. The not liking is the reaction. We have to be able to see this not liking or aversion that has arisen in the heart. We don't have to do anything about the busy mind. We don't have to manage it in any particular way. All we have to do is know the reaction that arises in that present moment right in front of our eyes. If we can see the reaction quickly, then the mind will cease making up more stories, and we won't remain stuck in our struggle or our pain. If we are not aware of the reaction that arises in the heart quickly or at all, then we will get caught in the reaction, continue to make stories and fall further and further into a painful struggle.

KNOWING VERSUS DOING

If our mind is very busy and restless, then normally what we'll try to do is find a way to calm the mind down. We will struggle, *"What should I do? How should I fix this?"* What we don't realise is that this not liking, this hoping it is different than it is, this trying to fix it—are the struggle itself! If we can instead notice that the heart is not liking the busy or restless mind, that the mind is not impartial to this phenomena, then the restless mind that is struggling will cease to be that way. It will become impartial, equanimous and will see that the busyness or the restlessness isn't the mind but something that enters the mind and then exits. It arises, and then it falls away. It isn't really anything of any consequence. When the mind becomes the stable observer of the body and mind, it will see that whatever object comes and goes is not us, is not who we are. Everything just arises and falls. This is what we are practicing the Dhamma to see.

Yesterday there were quite a few monks who came to visit me. A few of them have been monks for quite a long time. They said that their late teachers used to teach them about mindfulness. They taught them about becoming the knower or the stable observer of phenomena. When I heard them say this I knew that surely these were genuine monks from a long time ago. Unfortunately these days in the temple we don't hear this term, the knower or the stable observer anymore. Mostly what we hear about is concentration exercises, trying to make light appear or a sign appear in front of the eyes.

In the newer generations we don't hear about the knower or observer. We hear about the thinker or the story-maker; the one making up fictions and fabrications. Then what we try to do is control the mind so that it doesn't think or doesn't fabricate a false reality. No matter how hard we try, the mind will still think and make up stories. We end up thinking about how we are going to stop thinking instead of knowing the mind just as it is, with impartiality. If the mind is thinking we know it's thinking. If it's fabricating, then we know it's fabricating. If we can do this we develop a mind that is impartial to what is going on, and we don't suffer.

This is what this impartiality or equanimity means. The mind isn't involved in what's going on. It just sees it and is free of it. If we are not impartial or equanimous then we will end up thinking more, making more stories, and inevitably struggling.

For example, if anger enters the heart we know that anger enters the heart but if we don't like the anger then that means that we are not impartial to the anger. We struggle in a way, trying to get rid of the pain of the anger. We get angry and we try to figure out how to get rid of the anger. If we're looking for a way to get rid of the anger then the mind doesn't stop; it just keeps moving, keeps working. If instead, we're able to know what phenomenon is arising in the heart when it does, then the struggle stops right then and there.

KNOWING VERSUS FORCING

Many of us try to make the mind stop struggling by holding it still, trying to hold it and keep it as still as possible so that the mind won't shift into any negativity. What I teach is to become mindful of what arises in the mind. For example, if greed arises in our heart, if we can know that the greed has arisen and we know in an impartial way, then the greed will lose momentum and disappear right then and there. The mind will be an impartial one that doesn't suffer and doesn't continue making stories and fabrications which keep us in the pain of the greed. The more that we dislike a phenomenon that arises and don't want it to be there, the more suffering that we have.

If happiness comes, and we don't want it to go away, then we also struggle. We try and find ways to keep it. When we don't see what arises and we don't see the bias, the wanting, the liking or disliking, then the mind will continue to work ceaselessly. The more the mind is working, the more that it's struggling and certainly we will not be free from suffering in that manner. We won't find our way out of suffering in a pattern of fabricating endless stories and their resulting emotions. In reality, we can't force or prohibit the mind from disliking. The mind will dislike all by itself. We may wish or pray, *"Please let me be equanimous to all phenomena that arise,"* but it will never work. The mind is *annata*; it is not our self. We can't control it and choose what our mood, temperament or emotions will be. If we were able to control such things then the world would be full of enlightened beings, wouldn't it? If we had control of the mind, then why wouldn't we order the mind right now: *"Be enlightened!"*. Why wouldn't we do that? Simply, we can't because we are not in control of our minds.

KNOWING IS EQUANIMOUS

The mind will form, create or fabricate all kinds of stories on its own, and our job is just to know that the mind is doing this. We don't need to continue to fabricate more stories, the mind will do it all by itself. What we can do is to know that it's doing so, on time when the phenomenon arises. Simply by knowing quickly or on time, we won't be encouraging or perpetuating more stories to form. If we are fabricating stories, then we know in an impartial way that the stories are arising. The fabricating will cease temporarily. If anger arises, we see that anger has arisen. Then we want the anger to go away so we know that we are wanting. Then the wanting disappears. There may still be some anger left but there is no struggle against it. We are free. The anger can then teach us. It will show us that it is not the mind, but just something that comes into mind and leaves the mind. It comes in of its own causes and when the causes are gone, then the anger will drop off as well. It comes and goes and is just a temporary phenomenon.

The same is true of the pleasant and unpleasant feelings that come up in the heart. They come, they stay for a bit and then they disappear. They are not the heart. When the causes are there for them to arise, they arise. When the causes are no longer there then they disappear. We can't control this truth. Any good or bad emotional or mental state that comes in is just temporary. The state arises and then it falls away. It comes of its causes and it goes away when the causes are no longer there. It is not something that is under anybody's control. We see this again and again and one day the mind will have the wisdom that all happy, unhappy, good and bad states are temporary ones. Once the mind truly understands this, then it won't struggle anymore with whatever arises in the heart. The mind will be equanimous and will stop making fictions and stories and stop struggling. It will stop because it is equanimous. It will stop because it has wisdom.

Before we have this wisdom, when happy states arise we try to keep them. We try to hold them. When we see over and over again that happiness comes and happiness goes, eventually we gain wisdom into the truth. Then when happiness arises we no longer fight to try to keep it. We are aware that it's something that comes and goes of its own accord. There's no need to be enamoured by the happiness that comes up, to be pleased with it or to be displeased. Similarly when painful emotions arise in the heart, we usually try to get rid of them. We usually hate them. That's our old state of consciousness. Instead, we become skilled at seeing the pain that arises in the heart when it does. Seeing it come and seeing it go, we gain wisdom that it is just a temporary thing. Then our hate for our negative emotions starts to disappear, and we become impartial to the negative feelings in the heart. We won't struggle as a result of them.

EQUANIMITY IS A DOORWAY

If we keep watching and seeing the truth, then one day the mind will accept that all phenomena are temporary, and we won't struggle along with them ever again. Equanimity to all phenomena that arise and fall is the final stage of wisdom on the path of vipassana. It is the doorway to enlightenment. Once we reach that stage of equanimity to all formations, we have the opportunity to attain enlightenment and move from someone of the world to being above and beyond the world forevermore. From there we gain more and more insight into the Noble Truths, at more sublime levels of understanding.

For this enlightenment to occur, the mind must practice to become impartial and equanimous to the phenomena of body and mind. However, we must not become impartial through trying to control the mind, trying to force it still or trying to manipulate the mind into being impartial in any way. There is no chance of rising above and beyond the world if we're just equanimous as a result of practicing samatha or exercising control. The best that can happen from samatha is the arising of the occurrence of the jhanas, deep absorption levels of concentration. They are very peaceful but they are also temporary, and they are certainly not enlightenment. It's a totally different path.

In both paths, we can say that we are practicing to have the mind stop. In the case of samatha, when the mind stops thinking we get a deep level of peaceful concentration. In vipassana, when the mind stops struggling, we attain enlightenment. Those are the two ways of the mind stopping. Please let's not stop practicing the Dhamma: that's a stop that I don't recommend. That would be the most unfortunate kind of stopping.

Let's come back to our own hearts and practice to see the truth of the mind and body. This is where we will be able to find true and lasting happiness. We can have eternal happiness amidst all the pains and struggles and hostilities of the world.

Where we once used to feel lost and drowning, we can feel peaceful and happy. This is how amazing the Dhamma can be for us. This is the potential of the human being. Those who have never practiced true Dhamma have no idea or understanding of how amazing the human mind is and how amazing Dhamma can be. Those who practice and reap the results have nothing but love for their teachers and the Buddha who was the first teacher to show the way to end suffering.

The Buddha was able to teach us about something that is right here in front of our eyes, something that no one can see. Nirvana is right here in front of our eyes, but there are very few people in this world who are able to see the truth of it. Practitioners of the Dhamma are few in this world, and though a growing number, they are still an extremely small number compared to the vast numbers of people in this world.

Let's make an effort in our practice, let's be diligent and let's not do this for anyone else but ourselves. Let's not be lost in thought all the time. Instead, we must become aware of our body and mind. We must keep watching them often, and we'll start to see that the Dhamma is not so difficult.

A Conversation with Venerable Pramote

Student 2: My respects to Venerable Pramote.

VP: Hey, aren't you the girl who would always fight with her mother?

Student 2: Yes, that's me, but it's a lot better now.

VP: Good, good.

Student 2: I do walking meditation and I feel I have no energy, no vitality in my practice.

VP: Are you practicing in a way that you feel lazy or feel bored with yourself? We have to walk not in a tired way but in an enthusiastic way, a content way.

Student 2: I used to walk happily, but now I sort of know the phenomena but I don't really know. I feel as if I don't see phenomena sharply, and I am just looking at this and that aimlessly. My consciousness is just going out the eyes to see.

VP: When we practice walking meditation, we should not be looking at anything but our own mind. When the mind goes out to the eyes, we see that it went out to the eyes. We're not trying to be good in any way, not even to be a good practitioner. If your mindfulness isn't clear, then you may want to repeat the word *"buddho"* in your mind, when you're walking, standing, or no matter what you're doing. You can repeat the word *"buddho"* in your mind, and this can help bring you the stronger clarity and more freshness of mind that you require.

Student 2: Well, what I usually do is just move my finger most of the day. I keep my finger moving.

VP: Yes, but be careful that doesn't become too repetitive. For example, when I was a practitioner I used to set an alarm to go off every two minutes to remind me of my practice. It worked for a little while but soon it became so repetitive that I wouldn't notice it anymore. The mind gets used to it. Your mind has gotten used to this finger movement and so has stopped developing.

Student 2: Can I watch the breath instead of repeating "buddho"? I feel that's an irritating practice for me.

VP: Yes that's fine. Just be careful that what you choose is not boring and repetitive. It has to be something that makes us feel content and fresh. If we choose something that is too boring and repetitive, especially with your demeanor, a moody one, it will never work for us. You must find something that helps you feel more relaxed or content. Of course, dancing or singing won't do. Those things promote a very busy mind indeed.

Student 3: I feel so confused. I really can't watch the body or the mind.

VP: Do you know what being confused feels like? Sure you do. So if you're confused and you know that you're confused, that means you're able to watch the mind effectively. Now, do you want the feeling of being confused to go away? Sure you do. So just know you're wanting. There, that's watching the mind. That's how easy it is. So instead of thinking, *"What should I watch, or what should I notice?"* just know whatever feeling enters the heart right then and there as it does. Keep doing that. That's practicing the Dhamma. Has your mind gone off to think yet?

Student 3: Yes, it has.

VP: There, that's called watching the mind. We see that the mind go off to think. Watching the mind isn't stopping the mind from going off to think. Watching the mind is about knowing however the mind is at any particular moment. Has your mind gone off again yet?

Student 3: I'm confused again.

VP: And why are you confused? You're confused because you went to think, right? You see if we don't go off to think, then we don't get confused. Don't think too much. You're creating problems for yourself. You get confused, so just know that the mind is confused. That's all there is to it. You know what anger feels like right? So when you get angry, know that the mind is angry. If you want the anger to go away, then know that you're wanting. If greed comes in, and we don't want there to be greed, then know you're wanting there to be no greed. It's that simple. The mind will start to become equanimous.

Student 4: When the mind has mindfulness, I don't feel like it's heavy or light. I know that you've spoken before about how light mindfulness feels.

VP: And right now, would you say you have mindfulness?

Student 4: Well, right now I am noticing the heart beating. I would say yes I have mindfulness.

VP: Take another look and see if instead you're over-focusing. When we're focusing in, there will be a sense of stillness, heaviness, dullness. It will be rigid and there will be intention in the background, indenting to know and see. Instead know in a relaxed way without so much intention. Can you remember what it was like in the days before you were a Dhamma practitioner? The mind was cheerful and would change from this mood to that mood? Let your mind go, like you used to when you were a child. The only difference now, whenever any feelings come up, know they have when they do. Has your mind gone off to think yet?

Student 4: Yes, it has.

VP: Good, so when the mind goes off to think, know that it has. And now you're holding, trying to stop it from moving. Notice that you're holding. Doing what you're doing the mind will get too still and unnatural. Don't get disappointed or discouraged. When the mind gets disappointed or discouraged, just know that it has. See, feelings are coming and going all the time. Yet when we hold the mind still, we won't get a good look at these feelings. When we let the mind move naturally the feelings will arise and will change for us to see. A moment ago when you were listening to me you let go and let it be natural again for a moment. When you did, the feelings arose. There, now can you see? You became aware of the feelings, and now you feel happy. You feel like your mind is open and free, more expanded and bright. Do you notice that?

Student 4: Yes, I can see that. I feel happy now.

VP: Great the mind has to be that relaxed type of mind in order to practice correctly. How about now? Have you started to feel uncomfortable yet?

Student 4: Yeah, now I don't feel quite as comfortable again.

VP: That's because you started to control again. You started to hold the mind still again. You did that because you want to be good; you want to do something to practicing correctly. It's the wanting that's made it uncomfortable.

Student 4: Can I use the mantra "buddho"?

VP: Sure you can, but don't do that so you can keep the mind under control. Just use *"buddho"* so you can gauge when the mind is doing something else, like going off to think. There, great, what you're doing now is perfect! You see, you've become the stable observer. You can feel that the mind is bright and light. It can be seen on your face, you're smiling and looking bright. See the stable observer just lasts for a very short time. Then we move from being the knower to being the thinker. Then we may think for a little bit, and then we become the focuser or controller by trying to still the mind. Can you sense this? The mind cycles around between these things again and again. Watch the workings of the mind in this way.

Student 5: Right now I feel like the centre of my chest is very, very heavy and I'm also controlling things.

VP: Well, there you go. That's why there's heaviness in the chest, because you're controlling things. If you relinquish control there won't be that heaviness.

Student 6: I'm starting to see that the body is on a different level or layer than the mind is. Sometimes I can see that they are separate from one another and sometimes it's all just like one mass. I've seen this separation happen quite a bit over the last couple of months but I still feel like I'm not gaining any wisdom.

VP: Can you see that each of them are impermanent?

Student 6: No, I'm not seeing the impermanence of these things. Can I consider it? Can I try and think about seeing the impermanence?

VP: Yes, that's fine, use thinking to help you see the impermanence at first.

Student 7: Once I was walking and just for a quick second I felt like my mind was equanimous. But can equanimity be something that is seen by the mind, because I think I saw it?

VP: Of course it can. If you don't see it then how would you ever know you were equanimous? Did you notice that when this event happened that you weren't intending, that there was no intention in your practice?

Student 7: Yes, you're right. I wasn't really practicing at all.

VP: That's right, if we have intention in our practice there is greed, and of course if there is greed then we are not equanimous or impartial. Can you notice when the mind is equanimous, all things in the world lose their meaning, lose their importance? We have risen above the world, if for just for a moment.

Part Three

A MEDITATOR'S GUIDE

1

A Meditator's Guide

UNDERSTANDING THE PRACTICE

I t is a wonderful thing that so many of us have an interest in
meditation. However, before we get started with the practice,
we need to be clear about four key points:

- What are we going to practice?
- For what purpose?
- How do we engage in this practice?
- And while we practice, are we actually doing what we
intended or are we unknowingly veering off into some other
practice?

These four points are essential in directing our practice
in the right direction and keeping it from slipping off track.
They are the most basic type of wisdom in meditation practice,
called clear comprehension.

Whenever we meditate, there must always be two assistants present. The first assistant is mindfulness. Mindfulness is what sees or recognizes an object of body or mind, like the breath or an emotion. The second is the clear comprehension that keeps our practice in check. Without these two assistants, without seeing objects that are present and without being clear on what we are doing, it is easy to lose our way and falter in our practice.

SAMATHA AND VIPASSANA MEDITATION

There are two main types of meditation found in Buddhism: samatha and vipassana. In coming to the practice of samatha or vipassana, we need to have the mental clarity to know which one we have selected and for what purpose. The purpose of samatha is to bring a mind that is not peaceful to a state of peace, to bring a mind that is not happy to a state of happiness, and to bring an unwholesome mind to a state of virtue. In vipassana, we do not practice to change anything in this way, but instead, we practice to clearly understand things as they really are. We practice so we can see the true nature of body and mind.

SAMATHA

Samatha was well known and well practiced before the time of the Buddha. Before his enlightenment, the would-be Buddha learned from teachers who were skilled in the different levels of absorption concentration, or jhanas. Like most of us, he believed that if he sat in meditation that he would enlighten. He learned to make his mind very subtle and sublime. There are eight levels of jhana one can achieve. In the eighth level, the mind is so sublime that there is barely a trace of perception.

We can start by focusing in on the body or breath and make the mind subtle. We can enter the material or form jhanas from there, levels one through four. We can also focus in on consciousness itself and bring the mind into the formless realms.

We start by seeing the spaciousness or emptiness aspect, and enter the jhana of infinite space. We then realise that consciousness is aware of space and we turn our attention to consciousness itself. Then consciousness becomes aware of consciousness. The observing consciousness actually becomes the object of consciousness and this can regress infinitely. This is the jhana of infinite consciousness. After this, the mind can become disinterested in consciousness and the spaciousness. It enters the jhana of nothingness. Eventually the mind becomes so subtle that there is only a tiny trace of consciousness remaining: the jhana of neither perception nor non-perception.

The Buddha was taught to reach this state when he was still in his search but he found that when he exited the state, the impurities of the mind returned. He realised that samatha or focusing in on an object was not the way to get rid of the impurities or defilements of the mind. It is not the way to end the suffering in the heart of humankind. He realised that any type of meditation where we are holding to or focusing on a particular object, whether material or formless, is not the way to extinguish suffering. It is not the way to end one's karma.

VIPASSANA

Then after a period of body torture and denial, the Buddha-to-be finally found yet another type of meditation where the key is to be aware or highly conscious. He taught this way of meditation in the Anapanasati sutta or awareness of the in-breath and out-breath. In that discourse, he does not teach to try and hold attention at the breath and force the mind to be quiet or subtle. What he says is to know: to be aware and be conscious. If the breath is long, we should know that the breath is long. If the breath is short, we know that it is short. We are to stay alert and aware and know what states of body, mind or impurities of heart come in and pass away.

We must come to see this coming in and passing away of physical and mental phenomena in our experience. Our job then is to become aware of the body and mind regularly with an inner watchfulness. This is the practice of vipassana. When we practice in this way with frequency, wisdom arises—we come to know the true nature of the body and mind. This kind of wisdom is called right understanding. We come to know that the body and mind are impermanent, unsatisfactory and are not our self, not us. When we have enough wisdom to realise these truths authentically, consciousness can then let go of any attachment to the body and mind, and automatically comes to know nirvana, the end of suffering.

The body and mind were seen by the Buddha as five distinct groups called the five aggregates *(khandha)*. Each of which has the inherent characteristic of suffering (dukkha). If we practice watching the body and mind a great deal, one day we will truly see that the body and mind are just aggregates, elements of nature, fractions of the earth. They are not us, nor do they belong to us. When we see the truth that there is nothing we can constitute as being our self, we will reach the first stage of Buddhist enlightenment called stream-entry.

If we continue watching the body and mind carefully to the point of letting go of all attachment to them, then we become an arahant—one who has reached full enlightenment and completely ended suffering. An arahant is not someone who is able to make the mind something permanently good, or create permanent happiness or permanent peace. He or she is one who no longer takes interest in such things. Peace, happiness and the like are worldly endeavors. An arahant knows the futility in trying to pursue satisfaction through worldly measures. He or she knows the true nature of body and mind and is beyond any attachment to them. We need to practice vipassana to learn the truth about the body and mind that we consider our own. True liberation, the end of suffering, is not in trying to make the mind permanently happy or peaceful, but in seeing the nature of the body and mind as impermanent, unsatisfactory and not us—and then letting go.

THE THREE AREAS OF TRAINING

In watching and learning the body and mind directly, the Buddha taught that there are three areas of training: training in morality, mental training, and training in wisdom. Problems will arise if we don't train in all three of these areas.

1. TRAINING IN MORALITY

Many Buddhists believe that morality consists merely of taking a vow in front of a monk to follow a list of moral precepts. It is certainly not that superficial. For meditators, it is not only about adhering to lists of Buddhist precepts (of which there are five for regular laypeople, eight for nuns, 227 for monks and 311 for female monks). There is an entire other kind of morality we need to understand where we guard ourselves at the level of the senses. When our eyes see forms, our job is to be aware of any liking or disliking as soon as it arises. When we are aware in such a way, mental impurities or defilements (such as greed and anger) cannot affect us. Morality will occur in the mind automatically. Can we see how important it is to be mindful of what arises within our mind? It is necessary beyond the scope of meditation, and promotes moral behavior as well. Such awareness is something we need with us everywhere we go and at all times, for three reasons: for upholding the virtuous mind needed for moral behavior, for keeping the mind attentive and free from wandering, and for attaining wisdom into the true nature of things. So when our eyes see a lovely lady, and wanting and liking subsequently arise, have the mindfulness to see that desire has arisen. Once the mind sees desire arise, it will recognize it as being temporary, unsatisfactory and not itself. The mind will then not be at desire's mercy, and action in accordance with the desire will not follow. Consequently, we will not break moral precepts, such as pursuing a woman who is spoken for, or deceiving her in some way.

Perhaps we are walking and see a man's mobile phone fall out of his pocket unknowingly. As it turns out, it is not just any phone but the exact model that we were looking to buy! Greed and wanting arise, and mindfulness sees this. It knows right away that greed has entered the mind, and thus, the greed will immediately drop off and be unable manipulate us. As a result, we will not steal, even if we have no chance of getting caught.

If someone scolds us and we get angry, mindfulness sees the anger arise. Thus, the anger cannot affect us—we will not shout back, become violent or harm anyone in any way. The mind will be impartial. We will be moral automatically because of the mindfulness that immediately sees whatever arises in the mind.

The Buddha taught, *"...When your eyes see forms in the world, liking and disliking appear in the mind. Have the mindfulness to know when they do. If you don't see the liking or disliking immediately, the mind will be burdened and influenced by greed, aversion and ignorance."* The mind will stray from its normal state of purity and become immoral. A mind without morality is actually an abnormal mind. It has the mental defilements (greed, aversion, etc.) influencing it.

All meditators need to practice this method of morality. If

our ears hear we are being praised, liking arises and we become buoyant and inflated like a balloon. We must be watchful and know this as it happens. As a result we will be less likely to gloat and get mindlessly lost in the feeling.

Usually when we are on our own, we are in thinking mode: analyzing, replaying, projecting, curious about this, concerned about that. Some thoughts are about good things, some about bad things. Some thoughts create virtue in the mind, others vice. Have the mindfulness to see whatever appears in the mind as it arises. It then cannot override the mind's normal and natural state. This is when we can truly say that our mind is moral.

2. MENTAL TRAINING

The lesson in mental training is about the loneliest and neglected lesson there is. So few people are interested in learning it. Nevertheless, it is of such importance that the wisdom which sees the true nature of things cannot arise without it.

Most meditators don't take enough interest in learning proper mental training. Some just sit and meditate, thinking that meditating for hours on end and losing oneself in the object of meditation is proper mental training. This is not so. Others believe that it is enough to just practice labeling mental and physical phenomena, and the mind will become concentrated by itself. Once, again, proper mental training is not so superficial as to merely sit, meditate and hope for the best.

Mental training is about learning our own mental states —which states of mind are virtuous ones, which are not, which states of mind are suitable for samatha meditation, which for vipassana, and which states of mind are unfit for any practice at all. We need to know clearly the characteristics of each mental state. This way, we can see which practice is the most appropriate for us at any given time.

We must understand that there are two ways of learning. The first is the intellectual way, from teachers and textbooks. Those that learn the details of meditation in a scholarly setting will often find themselves studying the Abhidhamma. In this ancient Buddhist scripture, 72 conditioned phenomena are detailed, of which mind is just one. The mind, however, is the only one that can be separated into 89 or 121 different states. Though Abhidhamma is interesting, nobody actually experiences all these states. Learning in this way can be tedious and complicated.

The other way to learn is much simpler. This is learning the truth as it happens in our own experience. At first however, we do need to understand some principles, such as which mental states are virtuous and which are not. For such things, it helps to have a meditation teacher to point us in the right direction. Otherwise, we can fall into situations like creating unwholesome states of mind that we think are virtuous ones. This is surprisingly a very common occurrence among meditators. We also need to understand which mental states are suitable for samatha and which for vipassana. If we don't, we will likely bring a mind of low quality into our vipassana practice, rendering the practice ineffectual.

A vast number of meditators don't truly know what

samatha and vipassana are. They intend to do vipassana but actually unknowingly practice samatha. This is extremely common in all meditation halls. It is important to clearly understand the fundamental principles of each practice, and then all meditation centres will be of good use. One centre's practice isn't any better than any other; however, if watching the truth of body and mind is not a part of the program, there is no vipassana and no way to gain insight into our true nature. When we know the principles behind the practice, meditation is not so hard. If we don't know the principles, if we don't know about watching our body and mind, the practice will be very difficult indeed, like fishing for a needle in a haystack.

Let's have a look at what types of mental states are virtuous and which are not. Virtuous ones do not have desire, aversion or ignorance controlling them. So if in any moment the mind is wanting, is in a state of anger or stress, is lost in thought or lost in sense perception (looking, hearing, etc.), then it is surely not a virtuous or wholesome one in the Buddhist sense. This is an easy way to measure the quality of the mind in any given moment. With that said, sometimes we can't tell if the mind has desire, aversion or ignorance because they are there in such a subtle form. In such cases, there are other ways to know.

A truly virtuous mind is a light one. The arising of a weighty mind is a sure sign that we are faltering in our practice, that unwholesomeness has come in to replace virtue. Sometime our minds become so heavy in their practice it is as if they are carrying a mountain on their shoulders. A virtuous mind is also gentle and pliant. Any rigidity or dullness is not virtuous. Some of us have our minds held stiff all day long. A virtuous mind must be agile and nimble. We must be cautious and cognizant of such things.

We may notice that if we are too deliberate when we set our minds to practice, there will arise heaviness, tightness, dullness or inattentiveness. Why is that? It is because greed has entered. Wanting to practice is actually a form of greed. When we want to meditate we bring the wanting into our practice, and it will affect our mind. Normally when the desire arises to meditate, we meditate. As such, our actions are resulting from a state of mind that is defiled with desire, an unwholesome state. Heaviness, rigidity, inattentiveness and dullness will then appear. There will be no chance for a truly impartial mindfulness of inner phenomena to occur. Genuine mindfulness cannot occur at that moment because the area has already become a defiled one. Mindfulness can certainly never arise in conjunction with a defilement. We can only have one or the other. Therefore, if we are meditating and the mind is rigid or dull, know that this mental state has arisen out of greed. When the rigidity and dullness arise, aversion will also follow because we want these states to go away. We don't like them and feel confined and edgy. We want to be pleased, happy and comfortable. Once again, mental defilements prevail.

Let's come to learn the qualities of virtuous and non-virtuous mental states within ourselves. Speaking bluntly, almost all meditators are practicing without virtue, insofar as they are wanting to be virtuous. What they are creating is rigidity, dullness, heaviness, discomfort. Greed comes in; aversion comes in; but what is constantly arising is ignorance, and this ignorance goes unseen. The true nature of mental states like greed and aversion go unnoticed because ignorance is blinding us from it. When we practice by firmly holding our attention somewhere or intensely noting phenomena, the mind often ends up in a daze or just still and lifeless.

Sometimes, however, the mind does become gentle and bright, though what often happens next is that the mind becomes attached to the brightness, to the happiness or peace that arises. We lose our footing when this happens; we lose our way. This is a common trap for those of us who firmly hold our attention somewhere or intensely take note of phenomena as mentioned above. We find that the mind gets very calm and light. The mind is happy and shining bright. We must carefully notice that the mind is attached to the happiness and is stiller than it should be, more still than normal.

The truth is that the most suitable mind for practicing vipassana is a mind in its natural, normal state. A regular human mind is just right. Humans already are higher minded beings that are ready to uncover the true nature of things, to see the Dhamma. Nevertheless, many of us when deciding to practice forcibly hold our attention or mentally note phenomena until the normal human mind is lost and replaced by a subtle mind like that of a godly deity: serene, calm and blissful. Such a mind gets lost in these states and floats away in them. There is still desire looming, but because of ignorance we cannot see it.

These are some common mistakes of meditators. When

some of us practice, a non-virtuous mind arises: stressed, rigid, heavy and tight. When others practice and enjoy the beautiful sensations and mind states that come along with the practice, they get absorbed in them. When the mind experiences this, it is actually virtuous, but only in the worldly sense. We are actually creating an obstacle to the path of enlightenment in a very subtle way. We must be very careful. Some of us who practice in this way practice so much meditation that our minds become too subtle and serene, much more than is naturally so. We become immersed in such sublime states for days and days. Desire and ignorance have come in but they go unseen.

Some of us are able to hold our minds still for quite a while. Then when we come out of the stillness, we think we are great practitioners because we can successfully halt our mind and feel peaceful. The problem in this case is that no wisdom will develop. Such meditation will not wash the heart of the impurities that plague it: the ego and all the defilements such as anger, greed and delusion that keep us away from the Truth. After successfully holding the mind still, temporarily of course, we can end up with a heart that is even more impure with an even bigger ego!

In other cases, ignorance and aversion may be arising right from the start. This is especially true for beginners who practice by the method of mentally noting mental phenomena. By mentally labeling again and again, forcibly focusing attention each time, ignorance and aversion come in. We have to keep learning until we truly know the characteristics of the mind, and then we can practice properly without making these mistakes.

Then our mind will be an impartial one that can truly see and know mental phenomena clearly. This is a quality mind, one of virtue and wisdom. Such a mind arises on its own without any effort. In this type of mind, wholesomeness has momentum and fortitude. It is the most suitable mind for practicing vipassana.

Momentary Concentration

The easiest way to go about developing such a mind that is wholesome, that is a stable observer of body and mind and conducive to wisdom, is called momentary concentration. The way to achieve it is to choose an object like the breath or a mantra or phrase to mentally repeat. Instead of trying to make the mind rest and be comfortable and peaceful with this object, we observe the mind from this place instead. We keep this object as our main object and we set the mind free.

What will happen of course is the mind will go off to think. Then we observe or know the mind went off to think. Then the mind may go back and try to hold to that meditation object. Then we observe or know that it has gone to hold to the object. Then right away it might go off to think again. We observe or know that the mind has gone off to think again right away. The mind will oscillate between going off to think and going back to the object and trying to hold to it. We must observe these movements of the mind.

It's important to know that we are not practicing this to try to keep the mind peacefully with the object. If we choose the breath, we are not trying to stay with the breath. We are just trying to see what the mind does from this place. We start by breathing and then the mind goes to think. We know that it went to think. The mind goes back to the object, and we know it went back to the object. The mind goes to think again, and we know that it went to think again.

We do this over and over again and the experience of the observer or knower, the stable mind, that has this correct type of concentration will arise. Only it will arise just for a very short moment, each time that we notice that the mind moves out to think, see, hear or feel. When we observe or know the mind goes out to think, the mind will be the stable mind or the observer for just a moment. If we do this again and again, over and over, the experience of the observer or the stable mind will stay longer. The mind will be light and bright and comfortable and will be the observer of body and mind.

3. TRAINING IN WISDOM

Now we come to the lesson on the arising of insight wisdom which sees the true nature of the body and mind, or more precisely, physical and mental phenomena.

Once we achieve correct concentration, the stable observer, we can train in wisdom. This is the third of the three-fold training of the Buddha. Once we are the observer that has been developed through correct mental training, we will see the Truth. We will see that the body that is walking around, sitting, moving, brushing it's teeth, is just a mass. The body is a physical mass that isn't owned by anyone, and it isn't anyone.

It's not a person. It's just a physical mass that belongs to the world, that belongs to nature.

We will see that the body is one thing and that the consciousness or the observer that sees the body is a totally separate thing. We will start to gain wisdom into way that things truly are. We will also see that the mind with all the different thoughts and the heart with all the different feelings don't belong to anyone either. Feelings are just feelings, emotions are just emotions and thoughts are just thoughts. They don't belong to anyone and they aren't anyone. We will see this and gain this wisdom with the proper type of concentration.

We have to see the truth of this body and mind and eventually consciousness will release itself from this body and mind and be free. Even as we are still alive we will have no attachment to the body and mind. When the attachment dies, it is the extinction of suffering.

GAINING WISDOM INTO THE BODY

When we watch the body, we should not get immersed in it. The mind should be independent and watch from a distance as if we are watching someone else. We see this body stand, walk, sit and lie down. The mind is the observer. When we practice in this way, we will see directly that the body is not us. There will be no need to think about it; the body will be clearly and directly seen as not us or ours. The body stands, walks, sits and lies down and the mind is the observer. This is how to watch the body. One day the truth will show itself that the body is just flesh and bones, water, heat and movement. The body is under constant oppression by suffering, always in some form of discomfort. Then the mind orders the body to move or act to try to relieve the discomfort. When we practice correctly, we will see the true characteristics of the body for ourselves.

GAINING WISDOM INTO THE MIND

Watching the mind is easier than watching the body. When we watch the mind we will see that there are two things that arise in each moment: a mental phenomenon and consciousness. This is because one's consciousness does not arise unless there is an object of consciousness—they appear in unison. We cannot watch the mind without mental phenomena or emotional states because the mind has no body or form of its own.

First we should watch each mental phenomenon, whatever aggregate it is considered to be: a feeling or sensation, memory, or a mental formation. All such phenomena arise and fall in conjunction with consciousness. For example, at times we have a virtuous mind and at times we do not. Our impression is that the mind that belongs to us is now virtuous, or it is greedy, averted or lost in thought or sense perceptions. This is how we perceive it at first. Yet when the mind that is ripe with wisdom arises, it will see clearly that consciousness is one thing and greed is another. Consciousness is one thing and disliking is another. Consciousness is one thing and thought is another. They will show themselves as separate and distinct processes.

Consciousness will separate out from the body and will see that it's not the body but something else. Defilements or impurities like anger or greed that arise in the mind are also another thing. They are not the consciousness or the body, but rather they are another aggregate. If the mind is stable in concentration, then we are able to separate out these aggregates and see that none of them are us. Normally these aggregates appear to be stuck together like one mass. We think that there's a person. There will be memory that mistakenly remembers a person because there are all these aggregates are attached together like one mass, creating the wrong view that there's a person.

If we have a stable concentration and are able to separate out the aggregates or pieces, we will see that the feeling of happiness, unhappiness or neutrality is one thing, the mental formations like anger or greed is another, the body is another thing, and the consciousness that can see all these things is another thing.

If we can separate out these things it's like pulling apart a car. We can take the analogy of the chariot that the Buddha gave, and change it to a car and see that we believe this car is an actual thing but in reality the car is just a concept. If we split apart the car into its various parts, the axle, the wheel, the engine and so on, we can't say that any one of these parts is a car. When we assemble all the parts and they work together we conjure up the concept that there is a car. Similarly, we jump to the false conclusion that these aggregates are a person.

Let's keep watching and knowing the phenomena that arise in the mind. Doing this correctly, wisdom into the truth of all phenomena is sure to follow.

THE TWO EXTREMES

There are many mistakes, however, that meditators make which create obstacles to path of insight wisdom. We must not falter to either of the two extremes that block our progress in vipassana and in the arising of wisdom.

The first extreme is controlling our mind to the point of suspending it, making it frozen stiff or overly fine and subtle. The other extreme is letting the mind get lost, mindlessly following our ignorant and indulgent thoughts. We begin to practice the mind will either go wandering off thinking of this and that, unaware that the mind is thinking, or we will want to be good and practice well, and will hold the mind still or suppress it.

These are the two directions in which we can falter—total control, or mindlessly following the lure of the defilements. They are the two extremes. One is pulling in too much or controlling too much, the other is letting go too much and following the impurities of mind. Buddhism teaches the middle way. We need a certain understanding and finessing where we can find the middle way between these two extremes. Practicing the middle way is to know quickly when the mind goes out wandering towards impurities, following desires and following aversions that arise in the mind, and when the mind pulls in and goes in the other direction trying to be good, trying to control and trying to be still. Let's try to notice the mind that goes into either direction and then the mind will eventually find its place as the aware observer, which is the middle way between the two extremes.

There is a certain ability that develops though our understanding of the practice. Sometimes we need to pull in and control a little bit otherwise the mind will be out lost and wandering all day long. Sometimes we need to relax a little if we are over-focusing. To practice the middle way is to achieve a mind that is conducive to wisdom. Each of us requires a certain finessing based on our mind state at any particular time. Optimally, we want the mind to be neither too rigid nor too relaxed. Stable in knowing, and not doing, is the middle way.

GENUINE MINDFULNESS

If we want to know the Buddha's middle way in our experience, then we should gradually keep learning until genuine mindfulness arises, the automatic and impartial awareness of mental and physical phenomena as they arise in our experience. Genuine mindfulness will occur as a result of clearly recognizing mental states as they arise, not from holding concentration in one spot, or mental noting, or forcing it into being.

The Abhidhamma teaches that the proximate cause that enables genuine mindfulness to arise is the recognizing of mental and physical phenomena. When we first practice using the four foundations of mindfulness that were taught by the Buddha (namely, the body, feelings, mind and Dhamma or natural processes), we do so to achieve this mindfulness. We practice watching the body until we can see the truth of physicality. We practice watching feelings until we truly see the reality of feelings. We practice watching the mind until we come to know the truth of the mind. Genuine mindfulness arises on its own when we see the reality of these things.

PICKING A SUITABLE PRACTICE

Usually I teach my students to watch the mind. This is because most of us here are city people with busy minds. We are thinkers. Our jobs involve thinking all day so naturally, watching the mind is the most suitable practice for us. Those with a tendency to crave, who want the comforts in life and enjoy fashion and beauty should practice by watching the body.

Take a look at the decision to go to practice at a meditation centre. We don't think about what type of personality we have. We want to go, so we do. We don't notice our mental states. Our friends decide to go, so we go too. We unwittingly believe that if a meditation centre becomes popular, it must be a good one. The truth is it may or may not be. Furthermore, the master may be first-class, but if the practice doesn't suit our aptitudes and we merely follow the technique as directed, we won't accomplish much. So before we practice we need to observe ourselves and determine where our abilities lie. If we are the kind that is happy with worldly pleasures, beautiful things, comfortable surroundings, and like being left alone in peace and quietness, we may best suited to watch the body. This is because when we watch the body, we will easily come to know that it is not happy, comfortable or beautiful. Those of us who think too much, who are caught up in our heads, should watch the mind.

We should discern which of these two main personality types matches us best: sensual or analytical; that is, do our passions lie primarily with worldly pleasures or intellectual ones? Let the choice here act as a guideline for what our objects of meditation should be when we begin our practice. If we are primarily sense driven, we should watch the body, and if we are analytical, we should watch the mind. The other two areas to watch (according to the teachings of the Buddha on the four foundations of mindfulness, the Satipatthana Sutta) are feelings and the true nature of phenomena. We should not watch those two areas until our minds are a little more advanced, a little more ripe for wisdom. Watch the mind and the body first, as they are fundamental.

It is important to note, however, that watching body is most appropriate for those that are skilled in the absorption concentration levels (jhāna). Unskilled minds that concentrate hard will completely lose themselves in the body. For example, if we watch the abdomen rising and falling, the mind will be motionless and completely latched to the abdomen, thus rendered ineffective. In walking meditation, the mind will be latched to the feet lifting and moving. In watching the breath, the mind will stick to the breath so completely that we lose ourselves in it.

It is difficult to watch the body correctly if the mind is not firmly rooted in awareness, that is, if our mind tends to slip down into the object of observation. If we can reach the peace and higher concentration of the second jhāna, something arises that masters in the forest monk tradition call the knower or the observer. This observer is the awakening of right concentration, an unshakable awareness that clearly sees that the body, the feelings, the good and bad thoughts, and the mind that watches are all distinct and separate entities. The body moves; the mind is the observer. The body sits, and the mind is the observer.

If we have already been practicing a certain meditation technique which involves watching the body and/or the mind, I recommend we stay with it. There is no need to stop or change what we do. I do not teach a specific technique—we should continue with whatever style we do best and learn the principles I am teaching. When we understand the principles correctly, we should integrate them into our present practice. If the fundamental principles behind our practice are lacking or misconstrued, then it doesn't matter how gracefully we walk or how still we sit; we will not be practicing vipassana and what we do will not lead to insight wisdom. Those in marching bands have beautiful posture and perform gracefully, but we certainly don't see much enlightenment going on there! Our posture and technique is not the least bit relevant. We can just keep practicing whatever style we have learned in past, though we must bring a correct understanding into it.

THE FOUR SCENARIOS WHEN MEDITATING

If we have practiced watching the in-breath and out-breath, and we are comfortable with it, then we should keep at it. If we feel agitated, we may then want to pick another place in the body as a home base for our attention. Wherever in the body we may choose as our home base or primary object of attention, the mind will fall into one of the following four categories:

1) In the first type, we may be watching the breath, the abdomen rising and falling, or even an intentional body movement such as raising and lowering the arm. What happens is we get caught up in something and forget ourselves. Whether it is in dreamy states or peaceful sensations, we lose our awareness and mindlessly stray from our intended task. Almost all meditators who enjoy watching their breath get totally lost in it this way. This state is unproductive.

2) The second type occurs when the mind moves its way down into breath or other meditation object. Let us pay attention to our breath now. We will start to notice that the mind moves down into it. The mind that moves into the breath

is not one of right concentration, not rooted in awareness. The mind has sunk down. It is the same for those who watch the abdomen rise and fall or focus on other bodily movements: the mind sinks down into the area of attention. Watching the body standing, walking, sitting, and laying down can equally result in the mind firmly holding its focus. In this case, the mind sinks down and fixates on the whole body.

This is not a hard thing to do. It is quite easy to fix our attention on the breath, the abdomen, or on the whole body. Many of us are practicing by firmly fixing our attention somewhere. This is not the way of authentic awareness, not the observer we spoke of. Many of us firmly fix our attention on their mind, focusing as hard as we can until the mind is still. This is equivalent to samatha practice, and the effects of samatha will result such as tingly sensations, swaying, feeling light, or like our body is extremely large or floating away. Some of us mistakenly think when we experience such sensations that we are entering the path of insight wisdom. These are merely bodily sensations. The path of insight is about wisdom, seeing the true nature of things. So why is it that we intend to practice vipassana, yet we experience sensations associated with samatha? This is because we are fixing our attention somewhere, latching onto the abdomen or the breathing perhaps. If we keep at it, we are sure to feel lightness, floating sensations, swaying and so on. There is nothing surprising about this, as focusing attention in one area is the practice of samatha. It's not a bad thing to do this, but it is not vipassana. If ever our mind is so distracted and exhausted that it doesn't have the energy to do vipassana, then we can practice samatha. If we are skilled at watching the breath or the abdomen rise and fall, then we can gently bring attention there and feel calm and happy.

THE SECRET TO SAMATHA

The principles of samatha are not difficult at all. Normally our mind is restless and moving around, running from one thought to another, running from one object to another. It is busy, non-stop action and motion. For those of us who don't understand the practice, we will try to control the mind and make it peaceful or good. If we try to force the mind to be still, we will create tension. If we are forcing the mind to be peaceful, then we are practicing samatha wrongly. Not only are we not moving to vipassana, but we are not doing samatha correctly either. There is no stress or strain in correct samatha.

An important piece of knowledge is that concentration will not arise by forcing it to. Concentration is not the cause of happiness. Happiness is the cause of concentration. Try to remember this. Actually, as concentration gets more profound and subtle, happiness drops off and there is but equanimity—a sublime and wholesome state of complete impartiality. We don't practice concentration so that happiness will arise; happiness is what brings about concentration.

When arriving at the nature of things (Dhamma), often the cause-effect relationship between things will reveal that our previous notions were inversions of the truth. In this case of happiness and concentration, we can see that people who enjoy playing cards can often do so happily until dawn. The body and the mind are totally concentrated on the game. Those who like watching sporting events can get intensely focused on them and stay up far past their usual sleeping hour. They can do this because they are happy. The happiness brings them the concentration, and they stay focused on the game. This is how we should choose what to watch when we practice meditation: choose whichever object makes us happy. Whether our choice is the breath, the abdomen, or any other phenomenon, if we like it, it will quickly make us calm. Our mind will keep to the practice and will come to a rest.

If we know how the mind works, we will see that it is similar to a child, like a naughty toddler. It runs here, and runs there. One moment it laughs and the next it cries. One moment it is happy and the next it is upset. The mind is very much the same. If we force this kid to sit still and not let it move around, it will start to get stressed. The mind, if it is forced, will also get stressed. We need to find an object that the mind likes and then it will take the bait.

Let's say that the child in our example likes ice cream. When the child is running around outside, all we have to do is tell it to come in and have some ice cream. The child will happily comply. The child will not only stay put, but it will be quite content as well. Use this principle for samatha practice. We have to choose an object of meditation that the mind is happy with.

For some, watching the breath makes them feel happy. So they should choose the breath as their object. They don't need think about how to make the mind become peaceful. It is happy to be with the breath. Some people are content watching the abdomen rise and fall. So they should do this. Some like to walk back and forth. Some like to use a mantra like mentally repeating "buddho". Some like to make hand movements like in the famed Venerable Thian's tradition. Do whatever makes the mind comfortable and content. Happiness is the proximate cause for concentration. When the mind is happy, it will not run away from where it is. It will stay with the object it is happy with. This is the secret to samatha.

For those who say that no matter what they do, their minds never get peaceful, it is because they are trying to force the mind to be still. It will not get peaceful by doing this. We need to bait it with an object that makes it happy. When I was young I enjoyed watching the breath. I learned to watch the out and in-breath from Venerable Father Lee at Wat Asokarama in 1959. Most of you weren't even born yet. I felt happy watching the breath and the mind became peaceful. It was like a child eating ice cream. It was well-behaved. Let's use this principle for practicing samatha. We choose an object the mind is happy with, and it will become peaceful on its own.

Furthermore, let's be careful to achieve the correct restful state of samatha. We shouldn't get lost in a daze or dull the mind into a lowly, sleepy place and pretend that's what peace is. That's not peace. We shouldn't hold the mind still in a rigid and uncomfortable way either. We have to know how to feel relaxed and happy—and still fresh and alert.

When the mind becomes peaceful without any force, it is a stress-free mind. If we feel stress when we are practicing, then we can be sure we are not doing samatha or vipassana. If the mind becomes happy and peaceful on its own, without any force, then we have achieved samatha. Once the mind is happy and peaceful, it is not advisable to stop at this point. Just practicing to make the mind happy and peaceful is too superficial. Buddhism has teachings that are far more profound than that. Teachings on how to find happy and peaceful mental states are available without Buddhism and even predate Buddhism.

When teaching monks, however, I often advise them to practice samatha to get some temporary states of peace and happiness. This is because monks in general don't have the same outlets for happiness as us laypeople do. For regular laypeople, if we have a desire, a specific craving to eat or participate in something, we usually can easily go and eat it or do it and get some temporary pleasure. Monks don't have such opportunities. They don't have movies, television, or great conversations; they don't get to eat whatever they like and whenever they'd like it. Monks can practice samatha to feel some comfort and pleasurable states to get them through the day.

So far we have covered the first two types of minds that occur when practicing meditation, namely, getting totally lost, or losing oneself in samatha by fixing our attention on the arms, the feet, the abdomen, the entire body, or on the mind. What seem like many different meditation techniques from many different centres really just amount to the same thing: latching our attention on to something. Most meditators oscillate between the first two categories without ever being truly aware as in the third type.

3) The third type occurs when we watch the body as in vipassana meditation. We can choose any observable phenomenon of the body, such as the breath, the rising and falling of the abdomen, or intentional body movements. In the case of the abdomen, we can see that there is rising and falling occurring there, and the mind merely watches this. The mind must be the observer, an independent phenomenon from the object. The mind does not sink down to the abdomen but is rooted in awareness, and simply sees that the body has this rising and falling motion at the abdomen. Or the mind sees the body is breathing in. It sees the body breathing out. The mind watches the body stand, walk, sit and lie down. It watches the hands and arms moving and stretching and so on. It sees the body doing what it does. The mind is just the observer. The body moves and the mind watches. The body ceases to be ours. This body moves, but it is not us moving. The hand reaches but it's not our hand. It won't even feel like it is a hand. It is just a physical form moving.

When we see it in this way, there will be a lightness to all that we do. Yet when we see it as our hand moving, the mind carries more weight. Whenever the hand moves and the mind just knows it, there is tremendous relief. True mindfulness arises. The mind awakens and sees that the physical form that is moving is not us.

4) The fourth category is when we have been practicing the watching of an object of meditation such as in-breath and out-breath, and we are able to notice the occurrence of mental phenomena. Perhaps the mind goes off in thought, or the mind latches itself on the breath or the abdomen. We become mindful of whatever happens.

Here are a few more examples: We watch the breath and a feeling of joy or rapture arises in the mind and we immediately know that joy has arisen. We watch the breath and happiness arises; the mind knows that happiness has arisen. We watch the breath and feel anxious; the mind knows the anxiousness. Or we watch the abdomen and feel frustrated; the mind knows frustration has arisen. Whatever mental state arises, mindfulness is there to recognize it. As we practice this more and more, we will see how what arises in the mind is always changing. We will eventually come to recognize a great number of mental phenomena. We will know what getting lost in thought is like, what fixing the mind on a spot is like, what a virtuous or non-virtuous mind is like, what greed, aversion and ignorance are like. When we recognize such phenomena well, mindfulness will arise on its own in our daily life.

We can see then that mindfulness as described in this fourth case can also be practiced throughout the day. This is a little harder for those of us who prefer to watch the body, as the body tends to take up all of our attention when we do.

For those of us who are skilled at watching the mind, we can do this quite easily. As an example of watching our mind in daily life, we may see our friend coming towards us. When she does, gladness arises. Mindfulness knows this right away, even if we weren't intending to practice. Wisdom sees the gladness and it falls away. Phenomena just arise and pass away. We start talking and with our friend and start enjoying ourselves. The fun feeling arises, mindfulness knows it and then the fun feeling passes. Then our friend says something that bothers us. A little anger arises, it is known immediately and then falls away. If we can watch the arising and falling away of mental phenomena repetitively in this way, then we are able to develop our mindfulness in daily life.

The first category described is the mental state that most people are in all the time, lost all day and all night. There are six ways to be lost: in seeing, hearing, smelling, tasting, bodily sensations, and in thinking. There is one more way to be lost, actually, and that is the second category: lost in meditating, that is, lost in fixation on an object or in mental noting. We can enter this second mental state anywhere, but it is quite common among temple goers. They go on a short retreat and get very good at losing themselves in the breath or the abdomen.

The third and fourth categories can be accomplished without having to go on a meditation retreat. In the third, whatever the body is doing—standing, walking, sitting, lying— the mind keeps watching it repeatedly. The mind sees that the body that is engaged in these activities is not us. Such a mind is light and gentle, pliant and agile, adaptable and proficient.

Please try to follow what I say. If we read and listen to my talks repetitively our understanding will deepen. We will slowly absorb more and more each time. Don't just listen once now and come back a few years later and say it is all the same. We need to listen or read often so we will not forget. Please do keep at it. I won't force anyone to come. I don't charge for my lectures, and I give out my books and CDs for free. All I'm doing is asking us to come and listen, asking us for some determination and perseverance.

Now, the last few moments I have not been teaching about the true nature of things (Dhamma). Can we notice that our minds have a lot more movement? Our minds are much more active now. This is how we watch. We just know this is happening. It's easy. There isn't much to it. Most people have the perception that practicing the Dhamma means we must do difficult things, things greater or on a higher level than is normal or natural. If we endeavor to do things higher than normal, then we won't see the Dhamma. The Dhamma is completely normal and natural. We are not trying to become superhuman here. We are not even learning so that we can feel happy, or be intelligent, knowledgeable or worldly. We are learning so that we can see the truth. That is all.

It is not necessary to know all the Buddhist scriptures. No one does. We are not the Buddha. We just need to know what happens in our experience. Practicing the Dhamma is similar to climbing a mountain. Before we climb, we want to see what path others have successfully taken, and follow it. If we do, one day we will arrive at the goal. We will also believe that we chose the right way to get there. But standing on the mountain top, we then can see there are many pathways to arrive at the same peak. We could have taken other ways, practiced at other centres, we just needed to know the principles of the practice that I am explaining and thus get the fundamentals right. We need to know the four different categories I explained. The mind at each moment can be depicted as in one of the four, and only the third and the fourth are conducive to wisdom.

Watching the rising and falling of the abdomen and wandering off in thought or enjoyment is a futile practice, and is our first category. Watching by holding our attention at the abdomen is samatha, our second category. Watching the abdomen as merely the body moving, with the mind as the independent observer, is vipassana practice by watching the body. We will see that the body is not us. This is our third category. Watching the abdomen and seeing the mind—happy one moment, suffering the next, good one moment, bad the next—with the abdomen acting as the basis from which we watch the mind, is vipassana practice by watching the mind. This is our fourth category.

The same fundamentals are true for watching the breath. Watching the breath and losing our awareness will have no benefit. Watching the breath with a high degree of focus is samatha. Watching the breath and seeing the body moving with the mind as the stable observer is vipassana by way of the body. We will see that this body, now sitting here and breathing, is not us. Watching the breath and noticing mental states is vipassana by way of the mind.

For those who practice a style such as Venerable Master Thian's, where we sit and move the arms, the fundamentals are the same. Moving the arms with the mind wandering here and there is useless. The second way is moving the arms and keeping focus on them. Staying focused intently with each movement in this way is samatha. The third way is to know the body is moving with the mind as the observer. The fourth way is moving the arms as a basis for watching mental movement and mental states. The fourth way is how the practice was intended and originally taught, knowing the body is moving and knowing the mind is moving. Unfortunately most people don't follow the teachings and get stuck in the second state, and many more in the first, stuck or lost in thinking about each movement. "What step is next? Oh yes, this step. Ok great. What's next?" This is nothing but thinking. Even if we mentally note, "Thinking, thinking, thinking," we are still thinking!

Keep watching the different mental and physical phenomena. It doesn't matter which technique we choose. We all have our own ways; there is no need to copy others. Let's just remember well the three areas of training that I discussed. We learn by observing the eyes, ears, nose, tongue, body and mind. Whatever comes into contact with them, be aware as soon as it arises. Watch how the sensations are always changing. Observe the mind. Know what states are virtuous, non-virtuous. Most of us here are listening and feeling light; not in the "floating away" sense, but just gentle. Become aware of it now. Some of us are stuck intently focusing, fixing our attention. It will feel dull, sort of dry and emotionless if we are holding our concentration in this way.

(Venerable Pramote then takes the opportunity to assist an audience member) In your case, you are stuck in the practice of intense focus. You make yourself peaceful until you are in a kind of daze. This is not right. You need to be in a state of knowing, attentive, awake, self-aware, yet calm and relaxed. If you practice and you feel irritable or uncomfortable, the mind is not virtuous. In fact, these are defining characteristics of a non-virtuous mind. A mind that feels heavy is surely non-virtuous. A mind that is light or happy, however, may or may not be virtuous. Thus we must be careful not to be mistaken. Light or happy don't necessarily mean virtuous. Some people have light and calm minds all day and all night but are just lost, without awareness.

Please keep at it. What I said doesn't mean that the practice you are doing has been useless, but you need to keep working on it. Listen to me a little more and you will be able to practice vipassana properly. Most of us are stuck in samatha. We get attached to the sensations that occur as a result of our one-pointed concentration on an object, and think that we have reached a level of vipassana insight. Another name for vipassana insight is wisdom. Wisdom has nothing to do with physical sensations; it is about seeing the truth. This misunderstanding may be a result of some meditation masters of previous generations that would play little tricks to give encouragement and say that their students are reaching levels of insight even though they weren't. They were happy that at least the students made progress in samatha and they hoped that the students would then keep practicing. One day, by the grace of their merit, they may break free of samatha and enter the path of vipassana. Everyone please keep learning, keep practicing. Whatever technique we have chosen is fine. Each can be done correctly or incorrectly just the same.

I have practiced with many well-known masters of the forest monk tradition: Luang Pu Doon, Luang Pu Thaed, Luang Ta Maha Bua, Luang Por Phut, Phra Ajarn Boonchan, and Luang Pu Suwat to name a few. These teachers are unwavering about correct mindfulness practice. However, many newer disciples in Luang Pu Mun's lineage are caught in samatha practice—and not just in that lineage either. The lineage which watches the rising and falling of the abdomen is primarily composed of meditators who are stuck in samatha, stuck in holding their attention there. This is because many believe that mental labelling is equivalent to genuine mindfulness. This is a mistake.

Genuine mindfulness is about precise recognition, not fixing the mind somewhere and labeling it with a word. When we note in such a way, we are investing greed in our intent. Greed is continuously entering into our practice unnoticed. In the Commentaries to the Theravada Buddhist Scriptures it is mentioned that mindfulness by noting mental and physical phenomena carries suffering with it. Desire is hovering in the background, which is the cause of suffering. If we want to practice, and then start noting, suffering arises immediately.

The defilement of wanting to practice is the force behind the noting, causing further karma, further suffering. With that said, some who like noting phenomena are quite skilled and can do it happily. They start off with the defilements, producing further karma, and yet eventually settle in to a nice practice.

VIRTUOUS AND NON-VIRTUOUS STATES

It is possible that unwholesome mental states can cause virtue to arise. It is also possible that virtue causes unwholesomeness. For example, we see our child running out into the middle of the street or playing in the rain and we have compassion for our child. We don't want to see our child get struck by a car or catch a cold. So we call our child into the house. Then when our child refuses to come in, we start to get angry. What we say or do may hurt the child more than a cold would. In this case, we can see a virtuous mind soon produces an unwholesome one.

Once there was a well-known monk who had so much loving-kindness. Unfortunately, his love was so vast that it exceeded his mindfulness. This caused desire and attachment to enter at times when he wasn't sufficiently aware. If we have loving-kindness, losing our footing just a little bit can cause desire. If we have compassion, and our mindfulness is not strong enough, it may result in anger. So we must truly be careful.

Non-virtue can create virtue and virtue can create non-virtue. It goes both ways, as in the following example. We can be in the non-virtuous state well known as the wandering mind. Yet after an hour or so, we remember our mindfulness and recognize that the mind has been wandering. Now the mind has become virtuous, at least for this moment of mindfulness. We may then get upset with our mind for wandering away for so long, thinking, *"I can't believe that happened again!"* Now we are lost in non-virtue again, this time in regret and overthinking. Another common situation that occurs is when we are concerned about the future and the mind wanders away into different scenarios. Such a non-virtuous mind becomes virtuous the moment that mindfulness realises this is going on. Then we think, *"How can I prevent all this wandering?"* and we then proceed to feverishly mentally note the thinking. This is most certainly greed, and not virtue.

Please listen to this principle carefully: We are not practicing so that the mind will not wander. We are practicing to know ourselves, to be aware of ourselves. We need to see the wandering mind, to know what it is like, to see it is not permanent, and see that the aware mind that was lost is not permanent either. We are not even practicing so that we can be aware of ourselves all the time. We are not practicing to be or get anything at all!

A virtuous mind or an aware mind is not a permanent thing. We will clearly see that we cannot prevent being lost in thought. We can't chase it away, and we can't command mindfulness to come in. We also can't make it stay. Being lost or aware, greedy or not greedy, angry or not angry—they are all equivalent phenomena. A truly mindful mind does not value one over another. They all teach us the Three True Characteristics —that they are impermanent, unsatisfactory and that they are not us. This is the wisdom that will arise in our mind. Then we will come to know the true nature of things, that a mind that is virtuous and a mind that is not are just passing phenomena.

I want to emphasize that if we are trying to hold awareness, we are practicing incorrectly. If we are over-focusing and holding to the mind we need to let it go and see that it goes to think, goes to the eyes and the ears, and it goes to think again. We have to see that all the aspects are impermanent phenomena and that they are all arising and falling. We will know that we cannot control them. In the end, we will see that all things that arise, also pass away. There is nothing in this world that persists. There is nothing that we can force to happen. If there is a cause for something, it will arise. When there is no cause for it to be there, it will pass away. There is no self to be found.

There isn't anything in the world that is a permanent fixture, a self. Things simply come together temporarily and we believe that's enough to justify the existence of a person. However, when we see clearly, we see but the workings of components and no self at all.

THE ENLIGHTENMENT PROCESS

The mind that has reached this point of understanding will automatically become completely concentrated. When the mind is completely concentrated, it will see phenomena quickly arising and falling away. Then there will be just a few "mental" moments where the mind releases itself from suffering. For some who are very developed, there will just be two mental moments, that the Abhidhamma calls the moment of access and the moment of conformity to the Truth. At this point the mind is closely following the Noble Truth of suffering (dukkha). The mind sees that each phenomenon that arises is dukkha. However, it doesn't have any aversion towards the unsatisfactory nature. Instead, it has patience and is completely impartial. It accepts the truth that dukkha arises and passes, arises and passes. Other than dukkha nothing else arises at all. It accepts the truth so fully that it stops its struggle to avoid or chase away dukkha. After that, the mind lets go of its attachment to the aggregates of dukkha; which is to say, it lets go of its attachment to the body and mind. It flows back into the stream of pure consciousness on the noble path to freedom, and the defilements and impurities that previously covered pure consciousness are then lifted away by the noble path. This is why in the Buddhist scriptures it says that the mind is released from what was tainting it—it no longer clings. This process of enlightenment is all perfectly laid out in the Buddhist scriptures. It is surprising how its words of truth managed to be preserved for so long.

It is the defilements that cover up the mind. When the mind completely sees the true nature of things; that is, sees that aggregates which make up body and mind are nothing but suffering, the mind will release its attachment to them and be free of defilements. It is like a fully developed chick that breaks its way through the egg shell into the vastness of the world.

When the mind is let go of, it releases from the world

and the idea of self so completely, so fully, that it never attaches again. We can picture a clown that sells helium balloons, holding a huge cluster of them together by just the string ends in his fist. All he has to do is open his hand, and all the balloons are released in a wink.

OUT OF THE DREAM AND INTO REALITY

The truth is that most people in this world walk around with their minds wandering all the time. There is no awareness of it for their entire lives. Even in their next life, they are completely caught up in thought. They never wake up and notice it. How could they notice? Their minds are too busy wandering all the time! Let's look at an example:

Suppose each person in this room, including myself, was a bad person. Then no one here would be bad. Can we see why? Everyone would be equal. Comparatively, we would all possess equal amounts of goodness. Now if one member of the audience became a truly good person, then I would be a pretty bad monk! We would be able to clearly see contrasts. Similarly, in general, the minds of people are completely lost in sense perception and thought all of the time. They have no idea that this is the case, but all the while they are suffering from it. It is consistent across the entire globe: there is no mindfulness at all from birth until death. There are only a few handfuls of people who are awake. Nearly everyone is completely lost, but does not know that this is so.

We should therefore listen to the Dhamma regularly and one day our mind will awaken. All it takes is to be truly aware for but an instant, and we will know that for our whole lives prior to that point we had been lost, totally absorbed in content. We will know what being lost is. It is like our above example, if one person suddenly becomes good in a room of bad people, he will clearly see that everyone else is bad, and that he had been bad up until then.

THE MIDDLE WAY

If we are watching incorrectly, we will be lost in one of two ways. We will be lost in thought, or lost in focusing, fixing, forcing our attention somewhere. If we watch correctly, we are practicing what is called the middle way. We watch the natural workings of the body and mind. We see the body and mind as they are. The Three Characteristics, the truth of impermanence, unsatisfactoriness and no-self will then reveal themselves for us to see. If the truth is not revealed, then we are doing something wrong.

If we make our mind still, the mind will seem to be a permanent fixture. In doing so, we will not have the right understanding. We will not see the true nature of the mind. Everything else will exhibit the Three Characteristics, but the mind won't. To practice the middle way rightly is to know what is wrong. Practice by knowing physical and mental phenomena, practice by watching different states: knowing going off into thought, knowing forcing attention, knowing greed, knowing anger, knowing mindlessness, and so on. Let's keep practicing in this way and genuine mindfulness will arise on its own, and the middle way will too. We can't force the middle way to arise. We can't determine ourselves where the middle is!

Many people try to find where the middle is. Some try to find it in the middle of the chest or the middle of the forehead, or just above the navel. I am not sure what they are trying to find. The middle way cannot be found in the body. The middle way arises in the place where there is genuine mindfulness. The mind will have mindfulness when it recognizes physical and mental phenomena. There is no thinking here. We have to feel it. Vipassana is not about thinking. Those who practice mental noting, be very careful. If anger or another non-virtuous state arises, we must know so. The knowing is virtuous. To then proceed and mentally note, "anger, anger.." is thinking, which is non-virtuous once again.

We must simply keep watch. We watch the body and watch the mind. There is movement of the body, and the mind watches. There is movement in the mind, and the mind watches. We become the observer and see the Truth. This is what true meditation is all about.

DISPASSION THEN LIBERATION

When the Buddha enlightened, he brought forth the teaching of vipassana, which was not available elsewhere.

Vipassana is learned so that we can see the truth of the body and mind. When we see the truth of the body and mind, we become dispassionate towards ourselves and this world. The Buddha taught that when we see the truth, we become dispassionate towards worldly existence, and once we become dispassionate, we then let go of our attachment to the world. When we let go of our attachment, we are liberated. Once we are liberated, we know that this is so.

When we study the Dhamma, we study the body and mind until we are liberated. Once we are liberated, our job is done. We need not practice the Dhamma anymore. It is not like working in the world. In the world, we work to make money and spend it. Once we spend it, we have to work again to make more. In Dhamma practice, there is an end to the study of vipassana. Once we are completely free from suffering, there is no coming back to the practice. It is not like worldly things where we suffer again and again.

Let me emphasize that we must see the body and mind as they really are in order to become dispassionate towards them. Once dispassionate, we relinquish our attachment to them. Once we are no longer attached, we are liberated. Once we are liberated, we know that this is so.

Therefore, step one is to see the body and the mind as they really are. What is the truth of the body and mind? The truth is that they exhibit the Three Characteristics (impermanence, unsatisfactoriness and non-self). Vipassana is deeper than most people think. Most people think that as long as they are watching the body or the mind, that they are practicing vipassana. Just watching the body and mind is still samatha. It doesn't matter how good our concentration is or how skilled we are at making the mind peaceful. That doesn't liberate the mind from suffering. We need to see the truth of the body and mind.

A Conversation with
Venerable Pramote

VP: How are you feeling today?
Student 8: I'm feeling sort of still, neutral.

VP: Are you feeling that way naturally or are you controlling yourself? Is there forcing going on?
Student 8: There is controlling going on.

VP: Yes, you are controlling yourself and making your mind neutral and emotionless. That's how you've been practicing. Can you see what you are doing? Observe what the mind is doing, again and again. See? There is nothing that doesn't arise and fall. Every phenomenon that happens comes and goes. You feel good and comfortable and that's impermanent.

Then in comes feeling uncomfortable or suffering, and that's impermanent too. All things are impermanent and we study and watch the mind to see that all states are impermanent.

Student 8: I feel that my mind is more stable than it was earlier today but I feel tired, exhausted.

VP: That's correct, there's a lot of sleepiness there.

Student 8: I think I might be suppressing or holding, pushing something.

VP: Yes, you're suppressing some anxiety because you are afraid to talk with me. You're thinking ahead and then suppressing some of the anxiety.

Student 8: I can see that as I'm talking now I'm being a bit phony. I'm not happy about that. I'm not equanimous to it, and I'm not seeing it go away.

VP: We're not practicing to make things go away, we're practicing to see that whatever is there, isn't us.

Student 8: I want to see it that way but all I see is that things aren't going away, and then I get angry about that. I see that I can't control it.

VP: That's right that you can't control it. You still see that the body is something special, something that can bring happiness. But if your wisdom is full and you see that the body is nothing but suffering, you won't see it the same way anymore.

Student 8: OK, I'll keep watching in this way.

VP: Good, keep watching in this way and see that the body is nothing but suffering. There isn't anything lovable about it. The mind is also not lovable. It's transient, changing all the time.

Student 9: I've been listening to your CDs and practicing for over a year now.

VP: What are you worried about, what are you curious about? You're practicing just fine.

Student 9: I'm worried that I don't have the same energy and momentum in my practice that I had in the past.

VP: If you feel you don't have enough strength in your practice, then come back and practice some samatha.

Student 9: But I'm afraid of getting stuck and addicted to samatha.

VP: Don't worry about that. The only people who should worry about that are those who are stuck in samatha and holding focus on objects, and don't know they are doing it. Or, there are some groups of meditators that may know they are holding their attention somewhere but they don't see the satisfaction or contentment that comes up as a result of it, so they get addicted to the state. Make sure you don't force the mind too still or try to focus with too much force. The secret to practicing proper samatha or making the mind peaceful is to just breathe and relax, just see the body breathing. Don't worry that you're going to get stuck.

Student 9: But I was stuck in it before.

VP: Don't worry, you're not attached to this practice anymore. Don't throw away samatha. The Buddha taught us that the things we must practice and develop more than anything else are samatha and vipassana. So the buddha never told us to throw away samatha, and we shouldn't. Don't be afraid of samatha. Practice it correctly. Once we practice it and the mind feels fresh and energized, then we can walk the path of wisdom once again. We can practice separating the aggregates. Your mind is awake. You're a good practitioner, so go ahead and continue practicing.

2

The Ways to Wisdom

Many people think Dhamma is complicated because of all the different teachings and techniques available. On the surface, it certainly seems as though there is a lot of variation from one monastery or meditation centre to the next. However, once we understand the proper principles of the practice that the Buddha taught, and are developing well, everything starts to make sense. Everything comes together and we see that even among the apparent disparity and contradictions in different centres and techniques, that there is actually a uniformity to it all.

PRACTICE ACCORDING TO YOUR DISPOSITION

There are many ways to practice toward enlightenment. We can start with practicing samatha, making the mind peaceful, then walk the path of wisdom and see the truth. On the other hand, we can start by practicing vipassana and walking the path of wisdom to see the truth and then peacefulness comes later. Yet another approach is to practice the two at the same time in conjunction with each other.

Those of us who have a peaceful disposition, who like to be alone and quietly sit under a tree or relax are appropriate for practicing samatha before walking the path of wisdom and seeing the truth of the way things are. Such people are also more suited—once the mind is peaceful—to watch the body rather than the mind because their concentration is powerful and able to see the true characteristics of the body. Their minds, however, are also probably a bit unnatural, too still to see the truth of the mind itself. Those of us who are most appropriate for samatha or peacefulness practice are best at watching the body first.

On the other hand, those of us who are busy-minded people, like most of us here who are working, have lots of responsibilities in life, are busy doing this and that, who may get easily impatient or restless, and who tend to be full of opinions, would be better at doing a different practice. Busy minded people do best at watching the mind and heart first before going to any sort of deep meditation or trying to make the mind peaceful or still. Such people can skip that for now and go right into taking a look at the mind and heart and seeing their true characteristics. We will start to notice that each feeling that arises in the heart whether it be happiness or sadness or anger or frustration, is something that only lasts for a very short period of time and then goes away.

PRACTICING SAMATHA TO WALK THE PATH OF WISDOM

For those of us with a peaceful disposition, we can practice the first type of concentration, but we have to be a very good meditator. We have to be skilled at concentrating on one object, such as the breath or a mantra. In this way one can make the mind very peaceful and concentrated to the point where the mind gets very bright and light. If our object is the breath, we will notice the breath gets shorter and shorter as we are more concentrated. The mind then moves from whatever object it was focused on to using the light as its object. When the mind is concentrated and subtle enough, the breathing will stop, the thoughts will stop, body is no longer experienced, and all that will remain is bright light.

At this stage the mind has entered the first level of absorption or jhana. Once there is stillness and peacefulness here with the light, eventually the light disappears and all that is left is pure awareness and equanimity. That is at the fourth jhana. There are also four more formless jhanas for a total of eight (see page 98).

Once one comes out of the second jhana or higher, then the observer remains in our daily life for an extended time. It can stay as long as a week. The mind has samadhi and can use this samathi to cultivate wisdom.

A lot of people think that Buddha enlightened because he watched the in and out breath, but that is a fallacy. The Buddha had practiced the in and out breath and went into the jhanas in order to put the mind in a beautiful clear and pristine state where it was then able to gain wisdom into the truth of body and mind. It's not just by watching the breath that we enlighten. If we practice breathing in and out, it's a nice practice to make the mind peaceful but it's not enough for wisdom to arise on its own. There's more we have to do.

This first type of concentration was practiced before Buddha and he saw that it could make the mind very peaceful but is, in itself, not the way to nirvana or the end of suffering. He did see however, that this quality of concentration is useful to gain wisdom. We can enlighten or reach the end of suffering through gaining the wisdom that this body and mind are not us, and that this body and mind are nothing but suffering. Practicing samatha to reach these high levels of concentration is very difficult especially for modern people, but if we are capable of doing it, our mind will be in a very awake state—a very useful state to walk the path of wisdom.

In this state, however we must continue to practice when we return to the real world from these deep levels of concentration. We can then observe one's own body and see clearly that the body and all the parts of the body contain no self inside. We can see clearly that the mind and body are two separate things. We can also see that the emotions, mental states and feelings also are not us, but just things that arise in consciousness and then fall away. We can even see the consciousness that observes all of this isn't us either.

STUDYING OBJECTS WITH A STABLE MIND

We start to see that all the feelings that arise in the heart are not the heart itself, and that the thoughts that arise in the mind are not the mind itself. We start to see that the mind is not the feelings or the thoughts themselves but is really that which is able to observe the feelings and thoughts. In a similar way, those who are more peaceful and observe the body sitting, moving and walking around will be able to see that the mind is the observer of the body and that the body is that which is being observed. There is a subject-object relationship. There are two things: a body and a mind, and they are distinct. Similarly, if we watch the feelings and emotions that arise in the heart, we start to see that there's a mind, or that which observes, and there are feelings that arise and fall in the heart, or that which is observed. They are also distinct.

In this way, we start to separate out into components what we thought was one solid person. We see that there's a body and there are feelings, and then there is that which observes the body and the feelings. When our stable concentration and mindfulness get very powerful, we start to see that feelings arise and fall extremely quickly in the centre of the chest.

When our concentration is this strong, we see that the thought process or memory that arises to classify the feeling is something separate from the feeling. If it is regarding the feeling, it will arise right after the feeling. Sometimes if our mindfulness is very powerful, watching feelings arise and fall over and over, we will notice that the thought process or memory doesn't even have a chance to identify or classify what the feelings are. The process happens very quickly, and the mind just sees that things are arising and falling; that whatever arises also falls. It is no longer interested in the content of the thoughts and feelings, and it starts to gain wisdom into the truth that things are always changing.

Once we have attained this stable state of concentration, we can observe the body in detail and then that will lead us to seeing the mind clearly. When we watch the body with a proper state of peaceful or stable concentration, we will see that the body isn't us. It will completely separate out or even disappear. Then all that is left is the mind. When we properly scrutinize the mind we see the true characteristics of it. This is a powerful way to practice, but for many of us reaching high states of concentration is impossible, so we need to rely on practicing the path of wisdom thought mindfulness first and more powerful concentration will come later.

BEING CONTENT WITH THE OBJECT

If attempting to make the mind peaceful and deeply concentrated, we have to be very careful not to watch the breath or the meditation object in a serious way where we are trying to control the mind or to hold the mind still. There should be no stress in it. Rather we should be watching the meditation object in a very relaxed and gentle way. I practiced in this way since I was seven years old and I didn't meet my true teacher until I was 29. I feel that I wasted 22 years of just watching the breath and becoming very peaceful, but really not getting anywhere. For 22 years I was able to meditate and make my mind peaceful, but then through the work day I'd have a stressed and restless mind just like everyone else. I didn't like that, so I would go back to meditate and make the mind calm again. I would just go back and forth between peaceful and not peaceful. I didn't move forward until I learned how to attain wisdom into reality in order to liberate the mind from suffering.

If we are able to practice to make the mind peaceful, we just have to make sure to pick a meditation object that the mind is happy to be with and enjoys watching. If our mind likes the breath and feels good watching the breath, then we use the breath. If it feels good with a mantra then we use a mantra. Whatever we do, the mind has to be comfortable, relaxed and happy as we do it. Concentration or samadhi will arise not because we controlled it into arising or forced it into arising. Concentration arises because the mind is comfortable and likes being with the object. When the mind is very happy with something it will stay with it. It won't go anywhere else on its own. This is the attitude we need in order to bring the mind into the peaceful states of absorption concentration or jhana. We use the breath until the breath disappears and all that is left is light. Then we watch the light. Once the light disappears if we continue along that absorption path, then we achieve the state of correct samadhi—the stable observer—that is necessary for widsom. We achieve that observer in the jhanas, when we exit and return to the regular world, our mind will be the observer of all things. It will be able to see the body and the emotions, mental states, all the mental and physical phenomena as they really are, always arising and falling, not persisting and not a self.

LOW QUALITY CONCENTRATION

If we are not already experts at making our minds peaceful, and we are taught to watch the body moving or watch the breath, our minds are not stable in awareness. Instead, our minds go out to grasp and slip down into whatever object we are observing. For example, if we don't have a mind that is stable in awareness, when we are watching the breath, we will slip in towards the breath and be lost in the breath or get stuck in the breath. If we are observing the body, or observing the feet while walking, the mind will slide right down into the feet. It won't be the stable mind or stable observer of the body. It will get lost in the feet and attached to them.

When we have this type of concentration, we are not able

to see the truth of the way things are, because the mind is not in a stable, aware, rooted position. It's lost in the breath or lost in the feet. If we don't have a true peaceful concentration where the mind is totally stable in awareness, then the best thing to do is to watch the arising and passing away of the feelings and emotions. It's best not to try and hold to any specific meditation object but instead go right to observing the truth of the feelings, the way that they are.

WISDOM FOR BUSY MINDS THROUGH MOMENTARY CONCENTRATION

For those of us who are busy minded and cannot meditate to achieve states of peace, there is an easier way. Instead of practicing to make the mind extremely peaceful and entering absorption or jhana, we can practice a type of samadhi called momentary concentration. Through this method we can still achieve a quality type of concentration that is able to be separate from phenomena of the body and mind and be able to achieve wisdom into them.

The way to practice this is to pick a meditation object like watching the breath or a mantra, watching the abdomen rise and fall, or watching the body walking, sitting, standing. Only, instead of staying with this meditation object and trying to keep the mind still or stop thinking, we use the meditation object as the background and notice in the foreground that the mind goes off to think again and again, naturally. We don't try to stop the mind from thinking. We let it think as it does normally, but we notice that it is thinking. We start breathing in, and when the mind goes off to think, we know it. Then we are breathing out, the mind goes off to think again, and we know that again.

The reason we choose to watch thinking is because it is the activity that the mind goes off to do most often. Thinking is something we can surely become mindful of often because the mind will do it often, as long as we're not trying to control it. We can watch a meditation object and see that the mind went to think and then when it comes back to the meditation object, we see that the mind came back to the object. This all must be observed in a relaxed way. What happens is that each time that we notice that the mind went off to think, the mind has attained correct samadhi or momentary concentration just for that moment. Then the mind gets lost in thought again, or it slips down to take a good look at the meditation object and gets lost in the meditation object. Then we know it has gotten lost in thought or in the meditation object again, and when we know this, the mind is in the proper state of samadhi again for another moment.

If we practice this often and we are able to notice the mind go off quite quickly, then we have several consecutive moments of momentary concentration. Soon it will appear as if it's a continuous thing, that the mind has attained stable concentration. Precisely, however, it's stable just one moment at a time. Having many such moments in a short period, we will achieve a high quality mind with correct concentration.

Stable concentration can also be achieved if we are able to practice meditation until a bright light appears. Then we can know the mind that gets interested in the light and moves toward the light. The awareness of that movement towards that light will help to make the mind stable in awareness and not move out. Each time we notice the mind go off towards an object, whether it be thinking, the light, the senses, or anything else, this is a moment of mindfulness. When there is a moment of mindfulness that's able to see the movement of consciousness towards the object, the movement will stop automatically because the movement is caused by a defilement, namely greed. If there's mindfulness in the moment after the defilement, the defilement will disappear. Mindfulness and a defilement cannot coexist. Mindfulness is a wholesome state and a defilement is an unwholesome state. A wholesome and an unwholesome state cannot exist in the same moment. When the mind moves out and mindfulness sees this, the movement of the mind will cease and the mind will be stable in the correct type of concentration. Watching the mind in the presence of bright light is a way of practicing both peacefulness and wisdom in conjunction with each other. The movement of defilements may appear to arise and fall very quickly, so quickly, in fact, that each defilement disappears before it can be identified (as anger, a desire, a thought, and so on).

PUTTING SAMATHA TO USE

Who here has been able to watch the body and mind moving and working, whose mindfulness is strong and whose mind is the awake observer that sees the movements of the body and mind all day and night? If you can reach this stage then you know how tiring it is. You can see how hard the mind works. The mind works very hard, all the time. The body doesn't work as hard as the mind does. How many times a day for example does the body get hungry? It does maybe two or three, or five times a day, maximum. How often is the mind hungry? It's hungry for this or that object, hungry for a good feeling, hungry for information, hungry to feel calm and peaceful, and the list goes on.

We can see that the mind suffers in the sense that it never rests. The body is resting and yet the mind is going and going. It's tiresome. If we've never practiced the Dhamma then we won't understand what this means, how tired the mind is. The body can rest and feel fresh again, but if we don't know how to practice samatha correctly—which most of us don't—the mind never gets a rest. If we know how to practice samatha the right way, we can make the mind peaceful for a while and then bring the mind to a place where it can get some rest, whether we be with a mantra, the breath, or bodily movements. If we can't practice samatha successfully, then we will have to walk the path of wisdom all the time and won't have any rest for the mind at all.

If we're able to practice samatha, we give the mind a rest

for a short time and then we put the mind to work. Let's not waste the opportunity to apply such a good rest. Let's use this refreshed, well-rested mind to effectively watch the movements of the body and mind. If all we do is rest, then we miss a big opportunity. We become lost in a low value activity, and we sacrifice the opportunity for the most valuable thing, nirvana or the complete and total end of suffering.

If we can't practice samatha, then we listen to or read these Dhamma talks until we feel content and relaxed. This is enough of a relaxation to practice vipassana and walk the path of wisdom. In the old days when I was not able to practice samatha effectively I would pick up the Buddhist scriptures and in reading the suttas my mind would become content and peaceful and I was able to continue with my wisdom practice.

If we can't do samatha and we need a rest, then we choose something that we enjoy doing, something wholesome that doesn't tempt the defilements. We can read teachings or go into a natural environment and notice the trees or feed fish in the river. Simply do something that makes us feel relaxed and content then the mind will have had a rest or will even be able to then practice samatha more effectively.

I had a student who said that his mind was way too busy to practice samatha, and it seemed there was nothing he could do about it. I asked him what made him happy. He told me he enjoyed listening to classical music. I suggested that he listen to classical music until his mind was content and relaxed then to come back and watch the mind. We don't keep listening to the music indefinitely, luring the mind into dreamy and sensual states. We listen for an appropriate amount of time until our mind is happy and calm. Refreshed and relaxed, we then effectively watch our mind.

If we know how to go into deep concentration, then we should do it. If not, then we need to have some finesse in knowing how to give the mind at least a little rest so we can then be able to be mindful and practice vipassana more effectively. When the mind is not resting and working all day and night, it's a suffering experience.

Not only is the mind moving, working and changing all the time, but it's also not us, not under our control. It is a natural thing that cannot be controlled. We can't order it to be happy. Once the mind is happy, we can't order it to stay happy. When suffering returns, we can't prohibit it from coming back. We can't chase it away. Ordering wholesome states to arise doesn't work and ordering negative or unwholesome states to go away doesn't work either. We can't order any state to remain. The mind is not afraid of us. If we try to push away a negative state, it doesn't go away. If there's anger and we want it to go away, we get angry at the anger and we have double the anger!

Let's take a look at the truth and see that the mind and the body exhibit the Three Characteristics. The body and mind are impermanent, unsatisfactory and not our self. This is developing the practice of vipassana or wisdom.

INTEND UNTIL AUTOMATIC

The mind does what it does by itself. When the mind is seeing the truth and walking the path of wisdom, there isn't anybody doing it. Consciousness operates by itself. Many of us get confused and wonder if we should not do anything. Of course, to arrive at the state where the mind is seeing truth by itself we must start with some intention. Then eventually we drop the trying and allow mindfulness to happen by itself.

This type of samadhi is not a state where there is no thinking. It's a state where the mind is able to observe, scrutinize and gain wisdom into the body and mind in an unbiased way without becoming attached to the body, the mind, or the phenomena that arise and fall. This type of samadhi is not only the ideal state for wisdom to arise, it's absolutely necessary for wisdom to arise. We have two choices to arrive at the proper samadhi in order for wisdom to arise: we can choose to practice deep levels of concentration (jhana) or we can practice momentary concentration watching the mind go off to think and return again and again to a meditation object.

For modern urban people with busy minds and active life-styles, it is best to forget about trying to make the mind peaceful or still because we are simply not able to. Instead we should watch feelings arising and falling in the heart, watch how the mind is feeling at any particular time and practice this second way. It leads us to the same realizations—the Truth is the Truth.

When listening and looking at me now, notice that our minds are going out towards me. Often whatever object we are looking at, our minds will go out to it. When we have stable concentration we still see, but our mind doesn't go out towards things. It's rooted in awareness. It doesn't go out to become one or merge with whatever it is observing. The mind sees the body as being something separate from itself rather than being the body. It sees the feelings that arise and fall as being separate from itself, rather than being the feelings.

Let's watch this heart and see that one moment it's happy and the next moment it's unhappy. Let's notice that one moment it's being kind and the next moment it's being mean. Let's notice that all wholesome and unwholesome feelings change all the time, beyond our control. Let's practice to see the truth of the way things actually are and see over and over again that whatever feeling or emotion or mental state that arises, also falls. It's there for a bit, and then it's gone. Then there's a new state that arises, and then it's gone. We have to keep seeing this right in the present moment; that a feeling is here, now it's gone, and now a new feeling is here. The mind starts to accept that nothing is permanent; that everything that comes, also goes.

When the moment of enlightenment is about to occur, the mind goes into at least the first absorption level or the first jhana. This happens for all beings who enter into any of the stages of enlightenment. All enlightened beings then are at least able to achieve this level of concentration, but that moment of enlightenment could be the very first time that they ever achieve it, depending on the way he or she practices.

Enlightenment or nirvana can be reached from a variety of different ways but it always happens by seeing into reality. When we understand the proper principles of the practice in the way that the Buddha taught, we are free to choose whatever technique or strategy suits our abilities and our temperament. We can start with samatha and make the mind peaceful, start with becoming mindful on path of wisdom, or even cultivate the two together. Any way we choose, it will be the wisdom aspect that sets us free.

There are many angles from which wisdom can arise. We can see the Truth by starting by watching the body, the sensations or feelings, the movement of mind, or the natural processes, like how the mind and body interact. For example the eyes see, and then there's a feeling that arises in the heart. As a result, other impurities may follow. We may see something, then we like it and then we want it. We must learn to watch these types of processes. The Buddha's' teachings are not just to be listened to, but also practiced. When we do, we'll see the results in our own lives.

A Conversation with
Venerable Pramote

VP: Moomai, how are you doing?

Now, how many of us turned to look at Moomai without remembering to be aware of ourselves? Be brave enough to admit it! (Venerable Pramote acknowledges two people at the front) The two of you here are knowing correctly. You understand, right? All that is required for my approval of your practice is to know the states that arise, and to see the mind get lost at the eyes , the ears, in the thoughts, and so on. Just that is enough. Just that is enough for genuine mindfulness to arise.

Let's not let our practice slip. Even the world champion boxer doesn't stop training. No matter how much strength we've lost in our left hook, we should never stop training. If we like to use a mantra like "buddho, buddho...", then let's use it. If we are accustomed to watching the breath, then let's keep going. If we have trained in watching the abdomen rise and fall, then we keep at it. Just know as different mental states arise. Some days we are tired and lethargic. Some days we fall into samatha. Some days we separate out of the mental states and are able to see them clearly. This is how the practice goes. If we practice in this way mindfulness will arise in our daily life. *(Another student now addresses Venerable Pramote)*

Student 10: Intellectually, I know so much about the truth. However, when it comes to my practice, I'm afraid I'm just totally lost in desire. I don't have mindfulness. I am not aware. I keep thinking about what you teach and what you say, but I can't seem to do it right.

VP: Just knowing that at the time it arises is enough. Mindfulness is not us or under our control. If it doesn't arise, then it doesn't arise. We don't practice so that we can be aware twenty-four hours per day. We want to be aware so that we can know truly that non-virtuous mental states are impermanent and that virtuous ones are impermanent too. This is what we are learning. We are not learning to have mindfulness every moment of our lives, knowing in every moment. Perhaps you can see that if we were never aware of the body walking, then we would never know that we were primarily lost in thought while walking. But if we can be aware of the body walking, then as soon as we are we will see, " a moment ago I was lost in thought, and now I am not. Oh, I got lost again, and now I am knowing again." Both being lost and aware of body and mind are impermanent mental states; they come and go. We cannot control them. Eventually, the mind will drop both of them. It will not drop the state of being lost and keep the state of mindfulness. Both of them will be let go of. I believe this is the place of your confusion. Sometimes the defilements such as desire are in control. This is normal. It is good that you can see this.

Student 10: Well, I don't think it is normal in my case. I mean, I do see small desires come and go, but when it is the desire to develop in my practice, it sends me on a tangent. I keep feeling that it is correct to have such desires.

VP: It is easy for good people to stop doing bad deeds, but difficult to stop good ones. Can you see that when we love goodness it is hard to let it go? The Buddha said that it is hard for good people to do bad deeds, but easy for them to do good ones. And it is difficult for bad people to do good, but easy for them to do bad. So in your case, you are a good person, so it is easy to stop doing bad. As soon as you see any badness arise in your mind, it drops away quickly. See it, and it goes. Regarding goodness, it is a different story. You are a good person, so it is hard for you to let go of goodness. No need to be surprised by this.

Student 10: I always want my thoughts to be good ones. So I have this unpleasant wanting in the mind without being aware of it.

VP: The truth is that once wanting has arisen, it is not a good thing.

Student 10: I am not aware of the desire when it arises. I just think I'm doing something good.

VP: This is a mental state that you didn't know previously. But now you know it. Do you see that? Now it cannot fool you. Now something else will instead. Whatever we can know when it arises in awareness cannot fool us into becoming it or clinging to it. Whatever we don't know has arisen will fool us again. But remember that we are not practicing to achieve or receive anything. We just practice to see the truth that all mental and physical phenomena are impermanent, unsatisfactory, and are not us. And when we see this, we return them all to the world. Upon completely letting go, no feeling of responsibility will remain, even the one to be and do good.

There was a doctor once that told me he went to pay his respects to a meditation master. When he did, he told the master that he has mindfulness all of the time; all day long he is able to watch his body and mind without fail. The master then looked at the doctor, smiled and said just two words: child's play. The doctor said he was very confused, and so he asked the master if he was not in a state of mindfulness. The master said that he was not. The doctor then asked what the master's internal dwelling place is. The master then said he will refrain from answering that question.

From this story, we can see that mindfulness of the body and mind, right concentration, wisdom and such things are the boat on which we sail to nirvana. We are not practicing so that we can keep this boat. Gradually watching and knowing the body and mind more and more is the right thing to do, and will bring benefit.

Student 10: Another thing I would like to say is that I think this is great. When a thought arises and mindfulness knows it quickly, the mind won't start wandering off. Sometimes when I'm not aware enough and the mind already gets into the story, I become aware a few moments later and know that I was thinking. I just want to say that I think this is a good thing.

VP: Good. We don't practice so that we can stop thinking. We practice so that we can know when thought does appear. In this way, we will not start thinking aimlessly and unwholesomely. If we have some task to perform that requires thinking, we can think. But if there is no reason to think, we don't have to mindlessly fall into thoughts. When we are mindful, we will see that we cannot prevent the mind from thinking, and we cannot control the fact that everything arises and then falls away. All mental states are the same in this regard.

3

Life Beyond a Self

DEVELOPING RIGHT VIEW: NON-SELF

All beings in the universe are under the influence of ignorance or wrong view. For example, we believe that there is a self or a person. Some of us believe that there is a self and that this self is permanent. We may think that once this body dies then this self is reborn into another body. Some of us believe that there is a self but once we die there is complete annihilation, that nothing exists after death. Physicists often don't believe there is any life after death but if you ask them they will say that there is a self. They believe they exist but that this self doesn't last any longer than this lifetime.

Many people debate whether this self continues or doesn't continue after this life. This is what we debate about but when we practice the Dhamma, we see the truth that there isn't a self after all. We see that this debate about the afterlife is a futile one, completely based in wrong view because there isn't a self to begin with. If there is no self right here and now, whether we die and there is an afterlife or whether it's complete annihilation, is irrelevant. Without seeing the truth, all of us are just continuing to perpetuate and collect more and more wrong views and misunderstandings grounded in ignorance about the way things truly are.

We think that the body is something that is really ours and is under our control, and that the mind is something that is ours that we can control. If anybody asks us what the true essence of Buddhism is, we can answer with certainty that the true essence of Buddhism is about right view, the correct understanding of the way things are. That is what Buddhism is about. It's not only about correct concentration, or mindfulness. The reason we practice concentration and mindfulness is so that we can observe and understand things correctly, so that we can develop right view.

THE MIND CREATES A SELF

We think that there is a self. When we are born we are taught that there is a me, and this is my mother and father. We are taught in this way, and it's not a bad thing. This is our brother, sister, our house, our dog, our friends, and neighbours. This is my school, my university. In fact even ten or fifteen years after some of us graduate, we still feel like this is my university and we still keep a bumper sticker or an emblem of it. The self has made its way deep into our psyche and identity. Then of course we feel affiliated and identified with a certain group and it's 'us' versus 'them' in battles or competitions between different schools. As we get older, there are of course more things to justify and perpetuate this sense of self. We start our own family and take on our own profession or job. More and more things reinforce a sense of self. Some of us have a last name that is famous or displays wealth or status. If we belong to a social class, or political party, that class or party is deeply embedded into our psyche. These things blind us from the truth that in the deepest sense, there is no self. These things make us feel as though there is a me and there is a group or society that we belong to.

If we practice correctly, we will know that everything we say and do is always reinforcing or reasserting the self. If we're able to see and know what the mind is doing, we will see that the motivation underneath everything we're thinking, doing and saying is the need to reassert the existence of a self. Let's try to notice this.

My disciple Venerable Ah and I were once being offered food somewhere and he went to throw out a napkin in a garbage bin. He noticed that he felt he was cool because of the way he was throwing it in the bin. Even in that small movement a sense of self appeared. The self is even exerting itself while throwing out garbage!

There's nothing we hold dearer than our self. Once we

become the stable observer of the body and mind, we will notice that this body and mind are not us. When some of us see this, we get very shocked. We get scared, sad, and wonder, *"Who am I?" or, "Where I am I, then?"* This is because this truth defies what we love so much. Some of us get so scared when we see there is no self that we stop practicing altogether. Some of us cry. We may feel like it's such a shame to not have a me. We can't accept this truth because it goes against what we were always taught. The practice of vipassana is the practice of seeing that there really isn't a me. The real truth goes against what we have mistakenly believed to be true all of our lives.

I had a friend who wanted to practice meditation. I taught him to practice watching the body and mind. One day in his practice he saw that the body consists of bones. When he saw this, he became so afraid of the truth of what he saw that he stopped practicing. We need to have some perseverance because we need to get beyond these initial stages of shock and worry when we do see the truth. If the mind can become awake and be the observer, we must keep watching the body and mind. Let's not be discouraged or back down when we see that there is no self. If the mind gets worried or shocked, we notice this worry or shock. It's just a stage we need to pass through.

When we see that there isn't a self, the worry and fear that arise are just passing phenomena just like everything else. If we see this, then eventually the mind will become impartial to what it sees. We keep watching the body and mind more and more, and wisdom sees the truth more and more. It sees that the body is something that is temporary and that the body is oppressed by suffering all the time. We will also see that the body is just a mass of elements coming in and going out all the time. It's not a person, an animal, a being, a him or a her, a me or a you. Similarly, we will see that the mind is not permanent. It's always in a state of flux. Happiness and unhappiness are impermanent things. Any positive or negative emotional state is also impermanent. Even the mind that goes to see or hear, to think, all these states of seeing, hearing, smelling or thinking, feeling, making up stories—all of these states are impermanent states. We will also see that the mind is suffering, unsatisfactory and oppressed.

AGGREGATES CAN'T BRING HAPPINESS

The body and mind are made up of what are called the five aggregates. As we begin to see the truth clearly, we see that the aggregates are everything that we believed to be us. For example, the body is the first of the aggregates. It's more appropriately just called form or matter, because the body is actually an abstract idea. What's actually real in the world of form or matter in the first aggregate are the symbolic elements of earth, water, wind and fire. Each points to a quality of ultimate reality. Earth points to the varying degree of hardness; water to suction or attraction; wind to movement and fire to heat or temperature. The first aggregate includes all these concrete forms. Then there are the other four aggregates which comprise mind or mental phenomena. These are feelings, memory, mental fabrications, and the consciousness aggregate which is aware of all the others.

Again, these five aggregates constitute the body and mind, what we believe is us. It's desire or craving, which makes us cling or attach to these five aggregates and take them to be ourselves. These five aggregates are sheer suffering. Since we don't see that or don't know that yet, we crave these five things. We think we can be happy through possessing these five aggregates. We grab them and identify them as ourselves.

Whenever we practice and achieve the understanding that the five aggregates are nothing but suffering, in that moment we truly know suffering. Then consciousness has the opportunity to abandon the cause of suffering—desire or craving—and we realise nirvana and suffering ceases. We have developed the noble path or the path leading to the end of suffering. In short we have practiced until we achieve a true understanding of the Four Noble Truths (see page 73) all in one moment, the moment of enlightenment. The end of suffering is realised when all desire and craving has been abandoned and we see that the five aggregates are nothing but suffering in and of themselves.

We can see that the body and mind are impermanent. They feel or think one thing now and something else later. The characteristic of impermanence means something was there and now it isn't there. It comes and goes. The characteristic of unsatisfactoriness is that this thing that was there was oppressed by suffering. The characteristic of non-self is the characteristic that something requires a cause for it to arise. When the cause is no longer there, then the thing goes away. It's not under anyone's control; it's just a succession of causes. We see things arising and falling, one after another in succession and we notice the characteristic of impermanence. If we see something that hasn't fallen away yet, and it's oppressed by suffering and it falls away, then we see the unsatisfactoriness quality. If we see that we have no control over what comes and goes, then that is the characteristic of non-self: things arise according to causation. There is nothing we can call our self. There are simply things arising and falling. This feeling that there is a me, is just a delusion.

Let's watch our minds. When we see or hear something and there's a moment of interest, our mind shifts. Our heart flinches. We can't stop this moving. It's uncontrollable. The mind is not something we can control. The eyes see. We can't forbid the eyes to see. They are eyes and their function is to see forms and light. The eyes are not things we can control. Once the eyes do this there will be a shift or feeling in the heart, that we can't control or prevent either. We can't stop the eyes from seeing and we can't stop the ears from hearing. The nose will smell, the tongue will taste and the body will have tactile sense, none of which are under control. The mind will make up stories and pictures, and we can't stop that either.

Normally we don't see that the mind is thinking, or the sense organs are seeing, hearing, smelling, tasting or feeling because the mind is not of a high enough quality yet to be able to see that these things are happening of their own accord. Even practitioners, we only see these things on the rarest of occasions and for the most part we are perpetuating our habit of being lost in the world.

Let's study and learn to see the things that are uncontrollable. Let's study that which is not under our power to control. Let's come to know the movement of the body and the mind. We keep watching and knowing within the body and mind until we see that there isn't a self. Once we see this, there's no doubt: there is no self, there never was a self and there will never be a self. All the big questions vanish. Questions regarding fate, regarding whether there was a self in a past life, regarding what happens when we die, and what this self will be in a future life. All of these questions drop off when we realise there isn't anyone at all. We see that everything that exists arises out of a cause. If there's a cause for something to arise then it will, if there isn't a cause it won't. There is no person in any of this. There's no self, even right now. There isn't any need to figure out what happens to us after we die, because there never was a self to begin with.

WHAT THE ARAHANT SAYS

Many of us wonder what it's like to experience nirvana. We see that life as we think we know it is merely a dream but because we love the dream so much, because we love our self so much, sometimes we are afraid to practice. We fear seeing that there isn't a self. We think that if there's no self in nirvana, then why would we want it? We fear that we won't be satisfied with nirvana. Some of us would prefer to have a self and suffer.

The enlightened ones or arahants are peaceful in the sense that they are free of these five aggregates. They are free of mental formations and fabrications creating a deluded reality. They are free of anger and free of greed and all the emotions; free of painful feelings that arise in the heart and they are also free of attachment to body and form. They are peaceful in the sense that they are not burdened by any of these things, because they have released their attachment to the five aggregates. They have let go of them. Although the five aggregates still operate while the enlightened being is alive, they've liberated from them.

There's a story in the Buddha's time about a wealthy man who wanted to listen to a doctrine about the undying or the eternal self. Of course this is because the wealthy man wanted to know or have comfort in the fact that he is immortal. He was looking to find this type of doctrine. He heard that the Buddha was teaching about there being no self at all, let alone immortality. The buddha taught about freedom from selfhood. If there's a cause for something it arises. If the cause is gone it goes away. The Buddha taught that wherever there is a self there is suffering. The wealthy man couldn't accept or believe that the one who teaches such things would be the Buddha. He assumed the Buddha must teach about the Self and immortality. In truth, the Buddha does teach about immortality in the sense of un-dying, however this is undying in a very different way. It's the Dhamma that is undying. He didn't teach about a separate self that doesn't die. There's no permanent self according to what the Buddha teaches. The Buddha teaches that once we are free of the delusion of the self or of the "me", we arrive at or experience the undying truth, the Dhamma. We experience an everlasting happiness; an eternal happiness. The mind or consciousness and Dhamma become one. Nirvana is undying and it is the greatest bliss.

Let's gradually practice the Dhamma more and more. There was a self hiding in everything we have done up until this point. Our parents and society helped to lodge a sense of self in our subconscious. Our friends and everyone who we have come into contact with have helped to reinforce this deep into our minds. Everything that we say or do, everywhere we go has this self going along with it and is an expression of this self. We perpetuate this self all the time and reinforce its existence.

When we come to practice mindfulness and see truth of the body and mind, we see that there isn't a self. We wash away the delusion of there being a self. We come to the essence of Buddhism, the real truth, that the aggregates of body and mind that we thought were a "me" are just masses of suffering. When we are able to see clearly and realise that there is no self in the five aggregates, then we are a stream-enterer at the first stage of enlightenment. When we finally see that not only are these five aggregates not only not a self but are suffering in and of themselves, then consciousness releases attachment to the five aggregates and experiences nirvana. We experience the undying state, the unconditioned state, nirvana. The state of being a separate self is a state of dying, a place of mortality but nirvana is the state of undying.

As regular people, we are lost in the world. We are pursuing happiness through worldly endeavours, through relationships, through fun, status, material things and so on. In a way, we have to "pull ourselves out of the world," which means to become aware of this body and mind. We have to become aware and then be able to see the five aggregates (body and mind) functioning and doing what they do: seeing the body moving and the mind moving, the emotions arising and falling, from an indifferent or unbiased perspective, as the stable observer.

If we are able to become aware in such a way, then within weeks, months or years we are able to at least attain the first stage of enlightenment, stream-entry, where we fully understand once and for all that the body and mind are not us.

In the Buddha's time there were many people who followed the teachings of the Buddha and were able to attain levels of enlightenment. There's no reason why we're not able to do that now. We are receiving the correct teachings and are able to see the truth of the body and mind just the same. Let's see that the body and mind are not us and we can become a stream-enterer. After that, we can keep watching the body and mind and see that not only are they not us, but that they are nothing but suffering and we can become fully enlightened or an arahant. But we have to be determined and cannot be lazy. Being lazy won't get us anywhere. We have to be diligent to work towards seeing the truth as much as possible.

If we'd like to be able to go through this process of

enlightenment efficiently and quickly, we have to be skilled at watching our mind, which means seeing the mind go off to think and seeing the feelings and emotions when they arise. We need to change realms so to speak, pull our minds out of the world and become above the world. Then we move from one who is of the world, to one who is still in the world but not *of* it.

Learning the Dhamma with me, at first we might find it difficult to understand what I'm teaching. Nevertheless, I recommend that we read and listen to what I teach again and again. It only seems hard because there aren't many people who teach what I teach. It's something that we aren't accustomed to hearing, but actually the practice isn't too hard for a regular human being to practice. Continuing to read and listen to my CDs and downloads will help. In fact, before CDs were invented someone recorded one of my talks on a tape and just listened to the same talk again and again until her tape broke. But it was enough for her to understand the practice.

Once we are able to become aware of our body and mind, it's easy to see that this practice is really simple. It's just difficult when we struggle and search for how it's done. However, it's quite easy to see whatever phenomenon is occurring in our body or mind in the present moment. If we worry we're not doing it right, we can just see the worry. We see it arise, stay for a bit and then fall away. We can see the worry that comes up is something that is observed by the mind, and that it's not us. We see that every phenomenon exhibits that same behaviour of arising, staying and disappearing. There's really nothing to it. It's quite easy. It's only difficult because we struggle and our minds waiver and wonder, *"how am I going to understand this? How am I going to practice today? What exactly is the teacher saying? What should I do?"* We try to analyse and make rhyme and reason of it all. This is what can get difficult!

Instead of wasting time trying to analyse and making life and the practice difficult, just come to know or be aware of whatever phenomenon is going on in the present moment, right here in front of our eyes. If we're confused then know right here and now that the mind is confused. If it's curious, then we know it's curious. We become the knower of whatever mental or emotional state or behaviour is occurring in any particular moment.

If we practice by thinking, "Oh yes, this is impermanent," or "Oh yes, there is no self", this is not observing. This is not the correct practice of vipassana. Seeing the Truth in vipassana practice has nothing at all to do with thinking. Observing is beyond the scope of thought.

We can never liberate our minds from suffering by thinking our way out of suffering. The observer is beyond thinking. In order to practice the Dhamma, we need to have a mind that is totally unbiased. An unbiased mind is just the observer, the bare witness of what is naturally arising in the body and mind.

The observer doesn't interfere or change anything, either. It is just noticing what is happening in the body and mind, just as it is, naturally. Seeing things as they are means the mind is equanimous. The mind isn't busy liking or disliking different states that arise. It is not trying to fix them and is not interfering with them. It is seeing things just as they are. This stable mind is able to observe the truth of the way things are. It sees that what arises also falls; it sees that all things are unsatisfactory in that they cannot lead to lasting happiness; it sees that the body and mind are ultimately not under anyone's control.

The root of what we need to wash out of our hearts is ignorance, or not seeing or understanding the true and natural characteristics of the way things are. If the mind still thinks that there's an opportunity to gain lasting happiness through this body or mind in some sort of mental, emotional or physical state that is permanent, we will stay attached to this body and mind and we will suffer. Only when we are able to see truly, clearly, in our direct observation and experience, that ultimately this body and mind are nothing but suffering can consciousness release itself from suffering. As soon as we gain the wisdom that there is nothing worth holding on to, or nothing that can satisfy us, then we let go and are free.

The most important thing, regardless of whether we have listened a lot of Dhamma or not, is once we understand, we practice. We have to be very diligent in doing so as well. We can't just read or play an mp3, listen to these Dhamma talks and think that we'll get results from that. There are no short cuts in this world of Dhamma. We have to practice. It's completely just and fair. If we put in the work, we get the results. Everything arises out of causes. We have to put in the causes for fruition in order to reach fruition. Hopefully I have helped to plant the seed for you. Now it is time to train correctly and sufficiently and the practice is sure to bear fruit.

A Conversation with
Venerable Pramote

*Student 11: I want to be able to show you what is going on in
my mind in the present moment but every time I speak to you I am
so nervous.*

VP: There you go! Nervous is what's here in the present
moment.

*Student 11: I was doing walking meditation and was walking
very slowly with a lot of concentration but I found that I started to go
into a daze. I decided to walk quickly and naturally instead of slowly
and meditatively. When I did that I found that I was holding my
attention at the movement, pushing and focusing too much.*

VP: Well, you do have to hold yourself in the practice for
a little while, especially as a beginner. At minimum it's much

better to exercise some control than to totally lose yourself in mental impurities. So at the beginning we have to overcompensate with a little focusing and self control. It's better than being totally lost. If we try to have the perfect practice from the start, we will find ourselves lost in thought the whole time.

Student 11: I only walk a very short distance and turn around and walk back the other way. But even just for one rotation the mind goes off to think—bam, bam, bam, again and again. Is that correct?

VP: Yes, good. That is what we are looking to see. The more we notice the arising and falling the better. Can't you see? There is nothing that is a permanent self.

Student 11: Well, I see things go away.

VP: Right, you are seeing the discontinuity of phenomena. Once we see the discontinuity and are seeing things arising and falling, we have entered the practice of vipassana. It's the first of the vipassana insights. But not to worry there are nine more insights before we get to equanimity towards all formations, the doorway to enlightenment. We don't have to pass through each of the nine individually, however. Some come in groups.

There is nothing more worthy to do than to practice the Dhamma. I can say this with full confidence because I was a regular person in the world for a long time. I had everything that people in the world were looking for. I had a comfortable home with air conditioning. I had a comfortable car that was nice and smooth to drive. I worked in a comfortable job in a nice office. I had all the comforts and forms of happiness that people strive for but all of it was empty and meaningless. Eventually it gets old and so do we. We get sick and we die. So there are worldly types of happiness, sure, but they are all ultimately meaningless, superficial and incomparable to the happiness of Dhamma in which we understand the purpose of existence. In the world, as we continue to do things, we find that we get worse at them as we age. Our skills fade. But as we practice the Dhamma if we continue to practice as we get older we become better and better practitioners.

I studied with many of the old monks of the day. They were all in their 80s and 90s with the exception of Luang Por Phud who was about my age now. I could see that these elderly monks had so much happiness and peace in their being. When we see most elderly people in the world we can see that they look old and tired, often ornery. But let's not blame elderly people because they're not asking to be ornery or angry. They can't control it. Their minds are just that way out of habit. So any of you youngsters if you are already moody, then if you don't practice the Dhamma and become aware of your own mind, this moodiness will continue and become a very powerful habit. You'll be one of those older people who are ornery as well.

However, if we practice the Dhamma from now on, our minds get more and more beautiful and more and more bright. And this brightness radiates throughout our whole energy field. These elderly monks who have freed their minds from suffering have so much joy and so much happiness inside that when they tell their stories, tears of joy run from their eyes. Once I was receiving advice from Luang Pu Lian, an elderly monk, who saw me as a good practitioner. He looked at me and said, "You have to fight to the end. You have to fight to the end", and tears ran down from his eyes as if he was an old triumphant warrior looking back on the days of battle. So let's not be lazy. In order to free ourselves from suffering we have to do the work.

ABOUT VENERABLE PRAMOTE PAMOJJO

Venerable Father "Luang Por" Pramote is a monk residing in Si Racha, Chonburi, Thailand. He is the abbot of Suan Santidham Temple, which translates to The Sanctuary for Peaceful Dhamma. He is rapidly gaining popularity, being one of the most effective teachers of Dhamma in Thailand. He manages to relate the Buddha's teachings on meditation and Dhamma practice towards spiritual enlightenment (nirvana) in ways that are easy to understand and are appropriate for our modern, fast-paced society.

He teaches the Dhamma to avid practitioners looking to truly understand the middle way and to progress in their practice. Bangkok residents set out on an hour and a half drive in the darkness of the early morning to arrive before sunrise and line up outside his temple to get a good seat to listen to his teachings, express their concerns regarding their own practice and receive individual advice—a custom that has been coined "submitting their homework" for the headmaster to fine-tune or modify.

He travels tirelessly around Thailand and abroad, teaching and helping to wake up the minds people as he goes, in what is quickly becoming one of the biggest Buddhist enlightenment movements in recent times.

Luang Por Pramote became a monk in 2001 at the age of 48 after being an efficacious meditator and avid Dhamma practitioner as a layman since he was seven years old. He has had many teachers along the way, but considers himself primarily a disciple of Venerable Grandfather Dune, from North Eastern Thailand's forest monk lineage of Master Mun Bhūridatto.

MORE BUDDHISM TITLES FROM ASIA BOOKS

Specification
h210 x w148, 192 pages
Trade paperback
Publication: September 2013
ISBN: 978-974-8303-98-7

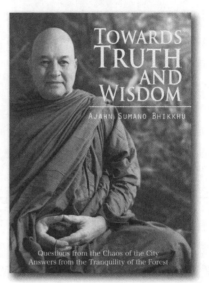

Towards Truth and Wisdom: Questions from the Chaos of the City, Answers from the Tranquility of the Forest
By Ajahn Sumano Bhikkhu

• Practical advice and solid instruction for those seeking spiritual guidance, suitable for Buddhists and non-Buddhists alike.

• An open, gentle forum of questions with honest answers that will teach you and touch you.

• A look from the Western view toward Buddhism. The author is speaking directly from the path to enlightenment, in Western terms.

In *Towards Truth and Wisdom,* Ajahn Sumano Bhikkhu, an American Buddhist monk, speaks and answers questions directed to him by spiritual seekers from all over the world. The basis of this book is formed from the earnest questions of these "city" people, and the profound, honest, and penetrating answers Ajahn Sumano Bhikkhu gives from his "forest" pespective gleaned from almost forty years of committed study and practice.

With a voice that embodies patience, compassion, and good humor as well as good sense, this book will awaken your wisdom and wise your heart on subjects such as relationship, sexuality, meditation, karma, rebirth, and death.

Ajahn Sumano Bhikkhu, born in Chicago, studied law and developed an entrepreneurial business before letting everything go and embarking on a spiritual journey almost 40 years ago. He was the first Westerner to be ordained in the tradition of Ajahn Chah in England. For 19 years he had lived in solitude and tranquility at his Double Eyed Cave Meditation Sanctuary in Thailand, where he still lives today. His books includes *Monk in the Mountain; Meeting the Monkey Half Way; A Deep and Perfect Vision: Dhamma Talks by Ajahn Luang Por Tate;* and *The Brightened Mind: A Simple Guide to Buddhist Meditation.*